HISTORY, PEOPLE AND PLACES IN EAST SUSSEX

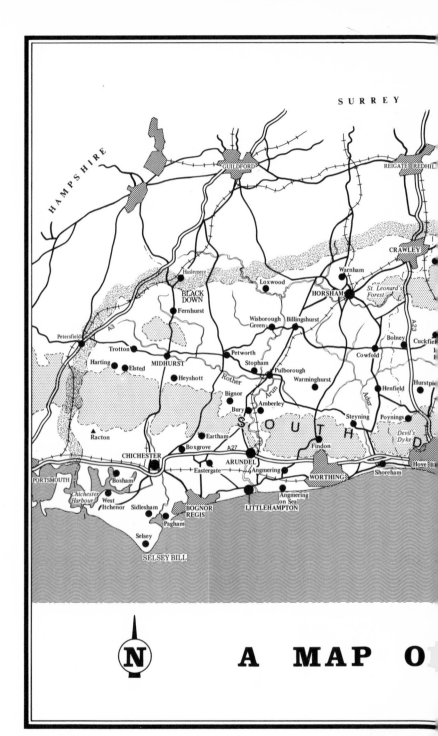

SURREY

HAMPSHIRE

GUILDFORD

REIGATE REDHIL

CRAWLEY

Warnham

Haslemere
Loxwood
BLACK
DOWN
HORSHAM
St. Leonard's
Forest
Fernhurst
Wisborough
Green
Billingshurst

Petersfield
Bolney
Cuckfie
Trotton
Petworth
Cowfold
A3
Harting
Stopham
MIDHURST
Elsted
Rother
Pulborough
Hurstpie
Heyshott
Warminghurst
Arun
Henfield
Bignor
Amberley
Bury
S
O
U
T
Steyning
Poynings
Adur
Devil's
Dyke
Racton
Eartham
D
Boxgrove
A27
Findon
CHICHESTER
ARUNDEL
Hove
PORTSMOUTH
Eastergate
Angmering
WORTHING
Shoreham
Chichester
Harbour
West
Bosham
Itchenor
Sidlesham
BOGNOR
REGIS
Angmering
on Sea
LITTLEHAMPTON
Pagham
Selsey

SELSEY BILL

A MAP O

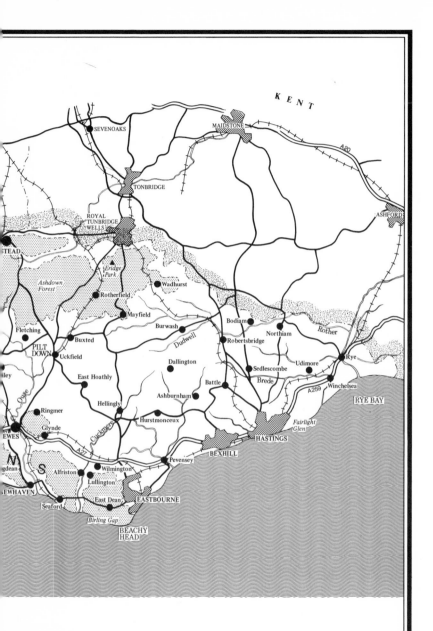

K E N T

SEVENOAKS

MAIDSTONE

A20

TONBRIDGE

ROYAL
TUNBRIDGE
WELLS

ASHFORD

STEAD

*Eridge
Park*

*Ashdown
Forest*

Wadhurst

Rotherfield

Mayfield

Fletching

Burwash

Bodiam

Northiam

Rother

Dudwell

PILT
DOWN

Buxted

Robertsbridge

Uckfield

Dallington

Sedlescombe

Udimore

Rye

East Hoathly

Battle

Brede

Winchelsea

A259

Ouse

Hellingly

Ashburnham

RYE BAY

Ringmer

Cuckmere

Hurstmonceux

*Fairlight
Glen*

EWES

Glynde

A27

HASTINGS

gdean

Pevensey

BEXHILL

Alfriston

Wilmington

EWHAVEN

Lullington

Seaford

East Dean

EASTBOURNE

Birling Gap

BEACHY
HEAD

SUSSEX

0   MILES   10

GDM

Mermaid Street, Rye.

HISTORY, PEOPLE AND PLACES IN

EAST SUSSEX

IRIS BRYSON-WHITE

SPURBOOKS LIMITED

Published by
Spurbooks Ltd
6 Parade Court
Bourne End
Buckinghamshire

ISBN 0 902875 79 5

Designed and produced by
Mechanick Exercises, London

Typesetting by Inforum Ltd, Portsmouth

Printed and bound in Great Britain by
Tonbridge Printers Limited, Tonbridge, Kent

CONTENTS

ILLUSTRATIONS

10

*Photographs by Richard Pike unless otherwise
acknowledged.*

INTRODUCTION

Whatever else may perplex me during the writing of this book, one thing is clear from the start. I believe it is an indisputable fact that the people of East and West Sussex are beings apart. Those who emerge from generations of unbroken East Sussex life on the rolling Downlands, in the secluded villages that still exist, and the busy, yet peaceful, farmsteads, have a different outlook on life from their brothers across the boundary. The eastern and western dialects are different, their cultures are largely unrelated, and no one could ever deny that the scenery in each half of the county is different.

The late Coulson Kernahan, whose home, 'Frognal', at Fairlight, near Hastings, was a haunt of literati and animal lovers in the twenties, wrote at length about Sheila Kaye-Smith, the poet and novelist who made East Sussex so much her own. He hints occasionally in his writings that she would never have dared to stray into the western territory. Steeped in East Sussex lore, she would have been the first to admit she barely understood the western side at all. This failing, if such, was never shared with French-born Hilaire Belloc, and, happily, one can record with confidence that East Sussex was almost meat and drink to Rudyard Kipling, whose delightful days in Rottingdean and at famous Bateman's at Burwash are mentioned later.

A more recent East Sussex literary devotee is Barbara Willard, who has lived in a cottage on the High Weald of forest and heathland for the past 20 years. In an article on her latest Mantlemass novel, Anna Pavord said in the *Young Observer* of September 22, 1974, that the East Sussex forest "has taken her over". Such is the spell the place exerts.

Bearing this in mind, and much else, it becomes clear that when, in 1865, the local government authority divided Sussex into two administrative sections, they drew the line to mark a fair division, namely, along the middle of the county, thus giving it the two county towns of Chichester and Lewes, with the cathedral city of Chichester taking precedence. Their deliberations did not create a division into eastern and western halves. They merely recorded something which already existed.

In those slow-moving, mid-19th century times, many difficulties were encountered in administering the county with the proper degree of efficiency. This was attributed to lack of suitable means of communication between the eastern and western parts of the long, narrow county with its five river mouths. Even in these days of electrified railways, it is probably easier for the Bishop to get from his palace at Chichester to Hastings by car via Brighton. Take any journey on foot around Rye. To achieve it successfully one needs, even now, both patience and local knowledge. True, the Romans made good roads, and could march about in almost any direction they wished. Our Saxon forbears, however, did not want to go anywhere, nor, for that matter, did they hope for anyone to come to them. One might safely assume that long lanes with no turnings were anathema to those Saxons. Thus, the difficulty of getting from one part of Sussex to another remained long after those chronicled times when, according to one much-quoted legend, the legs of Sussex women grew uncommonly long because of their practice of pulling them out of the clay-like mud! Although, by then, it might no longer be necessary for six oxen to be yoked to some old lady's coach to get her to church along lanes as soft and yielding as freshly ploughed land, yet enormous difficulties existed. It was not that the roads were terrible. They just did not exist at all. At last it was decided, in days when no Road Fund was available, that the only way to manage so unmanageable a county as Sussex was to divide it into independent, self-governing halves, although the drawn lines on the map may look a trifle artificial, it is, in fact, a very real thing indeed. Portslade and Southwick, so near each other, stress the point. The latter, in West Sussex, is surely an off-spring of the village green. The former, in East Sussex, is unashamedly what the Sussex author, George Aitchison, described as the "product of the gas-works". The respective residents still do not really fraternise. This strange conflict of life-styles and idealogies becomes neutralised further north in mid-Sussex, where the two strains can merge without rancour.

The 1865 statute of division was ratified in 1888, when the Local Government Act created the two administrative counties. These, with minor boundary adjustments, have remained until today, each with its own County Council.

Before the Romans came, East Sussex men were uprooting and burning the county's stalwart oaks and smelting the iron. This went on until the time of George IV, with countless traces of iron slag and cinders left to tell the tale. St. Dunstan had his smithy at Mayfield, and it was East Sussex iron from which he made a great pair of tongs. After heating them red-hot, he gripped the Devil by the nose so that the "poor gentleman" flew away to Tunbridge Wells, then in East Sussex, there to plunge his nose into a well and spoil the taste of the water for evermore.

It is sad that, as folk-lore tells us, neither devil, witch, warlock nor mischievous fairy could ever tolerate iron. This has sent nearly all the East Sussex Fairisees (fairies) to the western side of the county, which is where the poet, William Blake, swore he saw a fairy funeral while living at the village of Felpham in West Sussex for three years. While regretting that East Sussex was deprived of the great vision-ary's powers, it can be a consolation to reflect that, beside the lovely Felpham verses he wrote to the village, he also penned the following:-

The Sussex men are noted fools,
And weak in their brain-pan

Certainly not good poetry, it fully reconciles us to the fact that he chose to stay in West Sussex!

Turning briefly to the county as a whole, probably the earliest men-tion of Sussex is considered to be in 491, when South Sussex, or Suth Sexe, became an independent kingdom ruled by a Saxon warrior-invader called Elle (or Aelle), the victor of a large battle at Anderida, known today as Pevensey. Until 823 or 825 it remained an independ-ent kingdom. Following the Norman Conquest, it appeared in Dom-esday Book as Sud Sexe.

From the *Anglo Saxon Chronicle* we can discover how the name Sussex came into being. Under 477 it is given that the same Elle, or Aelle, with three sons, Cymen, Cissa and Wilencing, entered Britain from three ships at a place called Cymenesora. There, they killed many Britons, some being driven into a wood named Andredeswea. These places can be identified, Cymenesora is south of Selsey Bill, and now covered by the sea. The wood is no less than the Sussex Weald.

Bent on establishing himself in Britain, Aelle fought again with the Britons in 485 near an unidentified stream called *Mearcredes burna*. A third battle took place in 491, this time a very bloody one indeed. In the same year, together with Cissa, he besieged Andredescester, overwhelmed it and massacred everyone inside it. Thus, the great

15

Roman fort of Anderida fell at last to the invaders. Visit Pevensey and note that the Norman castle was built inside the Roman walls. This must have enabled the last Britons to herd together inside the fort, hoping to save the place. The fact that they failed, and endured such ferocity, is said to account for the depressive "something with an air of bloodshed" that still fills the historic ruins.

You may already be asking "Who was Aelle?" A fair answer is that he was probably Woden-born, and came from either Denmark or Germany. The former fact proves that he was descended from the Saxon tribes' god-hero. All English Anglo-Saxon dynasties traced forwards from Woden, and, deprived of that, they had no birthright of rulership.

In *Anglo Saxon England*, Sir Frank Stenton indicates that Aelle's conquest went from west to east, all British resistance being overthrown. About the probability that all the natives were killed, he has this to say: "The extreme rarity of British place names in Sussex points to English colonization on a scale that can have left little room for British survival".

Aelle proved himself a great sovereign lord. According to the Ecclesiastical History, he was King of the South Saxons. An interesting aspect of this title appears in the writings of the Venerable Bede

Aerial view of Bexhill with De La Warr Pavilion in foreground.

around 700 who lists English rulers who held the title of *Bretwalda*, of which a probably translation has been given as 'Britain Ruler'. According to the great ecclesiastic, *Bretwaldas* held sovereignty over all the southern provinces divided from the northern ones by the Humber River, and all related borders. Cissa succeeded his father Aelle. Eventually, their descendants declined in power until they were finally incorporated into Wessex.

In St. Peter's Church, Bexhill, there is a tablet linked with the rule of Offa, the great Mercian king, who, in 722 granted land at Bexhill to the then Bishop of Selsey. Eventually, England's sovereignty passed to King Egbert of Wessex. Queen Elizabeth II is his sixty-third successor. When, in 825, Sussex men submitted to Egbert, it was of their own free will, not through conquest. Even then, we note, they would "not be druv".

It is a good thing to remember that even before the patriarchs Isaac and Jacob lived in Palestine, the history of Sussex had begun among small groups of men and women around Eastdean and, to the west, Appledram. It was in East Sussex that Pevensey fell in 477 to the Saxon invaders. South Saxons soon settled along the foot of the Downs, then fanned out considerably along the coastal plain. Weald names such as 'hurst', 'field' and 'ley' are virtually our only records of that ponderously slow but sure domination of the mighty forest of *Andredesweald*.

Three centuries later, another great battle took place in East Sussex which shaped England's history for all time. Who has not heard of the Battle of Hastings, depicted in the glowing colours of the majestic Bayeux Tapestry? Although called Hastings, the battle took place some distance inland, and on the place where Harold died in 1066, Battle Abbey was built by William the Norman. Hastings Castle may have been a kind of Saxon stronghold, but was built in the Norman style, like, in West Sussex, Arundel, Bramber and Chichester, and, in East Sussex, Lewes and Pevensey.

These few facts have now set the stage for what is to follow. Born in the industrial North of England, I have long been identified with East Sussex, and feel spiritually akin with what, for lack of a better word, I have often called its 'gritty' quality. For me, man holds full sway in East Sussex. Wherever my travels have taken me from my Victorian home in Brighton's Regency Kemp Town, I have seen the results of ceaseless industry, far removed from rusticity and its sometimes enervating escapism. Modernity, of course, has caused some upheavals in the western area, but they cannot be compared with those in my half of the county. East Sussex, it seems to me, has

17

Post Mill at Argos Hill, near Mayfield.

always shouldered burdens willingly and efficiently. It has never turned its back on the responsibilities inherent in steady progress. For that reason alone, I feel honoured to try, however inadequately, to express some of the soul of East Sussex in this book.

Before local government reorganisation, the county of Sussex was divided into two parts by a fine line running roughly due north from Southwick to the Surrey boundary. This was for local government purposes with regard to County Council service. The area to the east of this line was administered by the East Sussex County Council, with the exception of that comprising the County Boroughs of Brighton, Eastbourne and Hastings, which provided all their own local government services. The remainder of the county was administered by the West Sussex County Council. East Sussex County Council has its headquarters in Lewes, the county town; West Sussex County Council functions in and from Chichester. The administrative county of East Sussex (i.e. the whole of East Sussex except the three County Boroughs) has an area of nearly 500,000 acres and a population of 441,550.

April 1974 witnessed notable changes in the map of England. Counties such as Rutland and Westmorland disappeared through being absorbed into larger ones with different names. Others, like Suffolk and Lincolnshire, became united. Sussex, fortunately, had a better fate. Outer boundaries of the geographic counties stayed unchanged, except for the transfer of a small area, including Gatwick, from Surrey to West Sussex. However, a new line now divides eastern and western Sussex, and a great part of mid-Sussex, including Burgess Hill, Haywards Heath, East Grinstead and Cuckfield, will have Chichester as the county town. Local government reorganisation has brought much further change to East Sussex. Now the new county incorporates the county boroughs of Brighton, Eastbourne and Hastings, all previously independent in their provision of local services.

Where a division between East and West has always been evident, their separation now is even more complete as neither will share a Lord Lieutenant nor High Sheriff. The Queen appointed the Most Honourable the Marquess of Abergavenny to be Lord Lieutenant of East Sussex, and His Grace the late Duke of Norfolk, after twenty-five distinguished years as Lord Lieutenant of Sussex, was appointed Lord Lieutenant of the new West Sussex, a position now held by his widow, Lavinia, Dowager Duchess of Norfolk. The High Sheriff of East Sussex is Captain Tom Egerton.

April 1, 1974, witnessed the disappearance of all municipal boroughs, urban districts and rural districts, and their replacement by fourteen new District Councils. There are seven of these in East Sussex, including three former county boroughs, and another seven in the western area. As the county boroughs disappear, as dignified Aldermen depart, and timeless boroughs and cities like Lewes and Rye in East Sussex (with Arundel and Chichester in the West) cease to exist in such guise, some will retain their identities as 'successor parish councils', or town councils. All in all, only the rural parishes have escaped the hazards and upheavals of what has certainly been the greatest administrative upheaval of this century.

Today, East Sussex has a population of some 660,000 (again, about the same as West Sussex), of whom at least 70 per cent live in the towns, mainly along the coastline.

1

THE FOREST RIDGES, WEALD, DOWNS AND COAST

The thriving area falls naturally and gracefully into four regions, lying roughly from east to west, namely, the Forest Ridges, the Weald, the Downs and the Coast. Being in greater proximity to London, the Forest Ridges along the northern flank contain a wealth of scenic variety. There, the busy development at Crowborough is only a handful of tree-edged miles from Withyham, where in 1663, the medieval Church of St. Michael was struck by lightning, then immediately rebuilt. Some 14th-century parts remain, and it is famous as a fine possession for a picturesque hamlet, with its Sackville Chapel wherein can be found the tombs of noble Sackvilles, earls and dukes of Dorset, who lived in Withyham before the family went to Knole in Kent. Why did they leave? The answer is both simple and amusing — because the roads were so bad! They can be seen, lying with their proud monuments about them, by Chantrey, John Flaxman, (favourite artist of the first great Josiah Wedgwood, known throughout the world as the "Father of British pottery"), Nollekens and Gabriel Cibber. A house called '*Duckings*', timber-framed, with close studs, reputed to be of 1507, stands near a hammer pond. This means that the house once belonged to an East Sussex ironmaster. Such contrasts, some picturesque, are typical of the Forest Ridges, a compendium of ancient and modern settlements, divided by natural woodland, plantations, or commons and stretches of scrubland.

The Weald, on the other hand, situated south of the ridges, provides contrasts of the same genre, but with somewhat different ingredients. Here, along main roads, and certainly cheek by jowl with railway stations, one sees residential villages and small towns. It is, today, a commuter's paradise. Numerous coaching inns are stocked with the bric-a-brac of past ages, and shine with horse-brasses and other gleaming tackle. While modernised cottages might make one think that the Sussex Saxon has retreated before the invasion of the developers and interior decorators, it is comforting to know this is

21

not so. The true Sussex man of the Weald lives away from the beaten track. From his remote villages and farmsteads, he trades in divers ways with those who have dared to invade his former privacy. He pursues divers crafts, as described in my recent book '*Sussex Crafts*', like trug-making, wrought-iron gates, thatching and shoeing hacks used by week-enders of the Weald. He advertises on rickety boards that he is selling "fresh farm eggs", oven-ready poultry, cut flowers, honey and jams, and fruits in season. If you seek a true picture of the Sussex man who still survives today, I can only recommend the writings of Sheila Kaye-Smith.

One of the most famous portions of the Weald is the Ashdown Forest, that natural jewel of heather, gorse and pine easily reached from most parts of the county, and now, fortunately, preserved for the nation. Denuded of its trees for smelting purposes during the Iron Age in East Sussex, it reached "from Kent to Hampshire, a distance of 120 miles", and was part of the forest known by the Romans as *anderida Silva*. It gave its name to *Anderida*, now known as Pevensey, which in those far-off days was on the edge of it.

Saxon man named Ashdown Forest *Andreaswald*, it being a part of the Wealds of Kent, Sussex and Surrey, which were all one. There are various interpretations of the word 'weald'. Some authorities give the meaning as 'forest', while others in contradiction give the modern meaning as 'plain' or 'a low hill' 'a region without woods'. One gazetteer of place-names described the weald as "a wooded district of Kent, Surrey and Sussex". It would appear that, originally, the entire area must have been impassably wooded, but with some open heathland dotted around, and lying roughly "between the ragstone ridge south of Maidstone and a line drawn from Ashurst to Dungeness, excluding the marshes within six to eight miles of the sea."

An interesting reflection on the Weald of East Sussex can be found in a splendid 1946 publication, *Tomorrow in East Sussex: A Contribution by the Sussex Rural Community Council towards Post-War Planning*. It says:

"We believe that for the purist, and strictly, the Weald of East Sussex excludes a part of the East Sussex countryside north of a line drawn east and west through Crowborough; and the dictionary says that the weald is 'a district comprising portions of Kent and Sussex, extending from Folkstone Hill near the Straits of Dover to Beachy Head'; but the dictionary also says that *weald* is 'any open country'. It is that which we wish to preserve — the East Sussex open and cultivated countryside, woodlands, streams and rivers."

22

Harvesting with horses on the Downs in Victorian times.

Now, we turn to the velvety Downs, on which the population tends to thin out. Here, villages fail to make contact with mushrooming houses. If one studies the barrows and encampments on these undulating hills, this part of East Sussex, and West as well, appears to be no more populated today than it was in the time of Iron Age man. In most of the villages, the people are still country-steeped workers. They breathe the champagne Downland air, walk tall across some of the most green and lush turf in England, listen to countless bird-songs without the interference of transistors, see rare flowers, and go along the ridge-walks where only sheep stare inquisitively at passers-by. The Ouse and Cuckmere rivers meander between the Downs, their valleys providing shelter for the region's inhabitants.

Having lived for so long in East Sussex, I tend to regard the Downs as only belonging to the eastern side! That, of course, is foolish impertinence.

Westmeston, Near Ditchling, is a typical Downland village, whose church once boasted a Norman wall painting. Similar minor work once existed at Western Slaugham, but both examples have now perished. Instances of very superb standard Norman wall painting exist at Hardham and Clayton in the west, whose famous windmills Jack and Jill, are described, with others, later. Tenth-century Bishopstone has a preserved south *porticus*, and like Arlington, has long-and-short quoins, or external angles of buildings.

23

Often, from the breezy, cloud-capped hill-tops, I have caught silvery glimpses of the East Sussex rivers that wind gracefully inland. The three western ones, the Lavant, Arun and Adur, can claim, respectively, a cathedral, a fairy-tale Norman castle, and Shoreham, with its busy port. In East Sussex, the Ouse makes a gap between the easternmost range of the Downs and the middle portion extending from the Ouse to the Adur. It is a fine river, with Lewes as its main town and Newhaven as its harbour and focal point. One of its arms is still known as the Iron River, a name that bespeaks the Middle Ages when the Ashdown Forest was in danger of becoming a Black Country through iron-smelting.

Compared with these, the Cuckmere is a slender thread of water that slips nonchalantly into the sea at Cuckmere Haven, more resembling a brook than a river as it curls and twists through the valley. As for the Rother, sited alongside the Kent border, it is the fifth river to divide the county neatly, and is far more utilitarian. In short, it produces a section of the Kent-Sussex boundary before it swoops back to Rye, lured by the prospect of a once-good harbour.

There are, of course, other rivers in Sussex, such as the Western or Little Rother, the Brede, the Ashburn, the Chilt and the Stor. Even the Medway rises in Sussex near Turner's Hill, 1½ miles south-south-west of Crawley Down. Finally, for good measure, there is a tiny river outside Brighton which runs underground, like the Fleet River in London, but which, now and then, breaks out of its man-made bonds, and has to be pumped back into oblivion!

Wonderfully, there are lofty places in Sussex where one can see the five principal rivers meandering to the chalk-girt sea. The best spot is perhaps on the road out of Friston, high above where Exceat once existed. From that altitude, the Cuckmere seems to be standing still on the floor of the green valley below.

Wandering high on the East Sussex section of the Downs often grants a glorious glimpse westwards of the Devil's Dyke, then comes the shoulder of Wolstonbury, which completes a view of the central area, and the noble coronet of beech trees on the brooding brow of Chanctonbury guides the eye to dimming western horizons. In the middle distance, Ditchling can be seen, with its common, winding high street and ancient aura, where artists live and reign supreme, and where singer Vera Lynn has her hill-side home across grassland facing the road from Brighton.

There may be some who do not know the legend connected with the Devil's Dyke, that sinister valley among the rounded Downs near Brighton. It was, so relates ancient lore, made by the Devil's spade, digging frantically in the hope that he would let in the sea onto the Weald and drown its thousand or more Christian churches. A sentence here must recall the epithet "Silly Sussex", the first word being nothing more than a degenerate pronunciation of the Saxon *selig*, or holy. It was because Sussex was so holy that the Devil was frustrated by an old woman who lit her candle to find out what all the digging uproar was about. This false dawn sent Lucifer scuttling away from the Downs for ever.

Over at Beachy Head, the East Sussex Downs meet the sea, though not only there, for cliffs dominate the coastal scene from the towering 575 feet of chalk which makes a back-cloth for the 20th-century lighthouse at its foot, with its 40,000 candle-power lamp and ray visible for over 20 miles. Who, wandering over this part of the Downs, which houses Kipling's former famous home, Bateman's, at Burwash, now owned by the nation, has not seen Brightling Needle, standing on Brightling Down at a height of 646 feet, together with the domed temple in Brightling Park behind a long screen of beeches, and the Sugar-Loaf near the road from Heathfield to Battle near Woods Corner? All these were built by a wealthy East Sussex eccentric called Jack Fuller, of Rose Hill, who died in 1834, aged seventy-seven. It is said that on a clear day France can be seen from the obelisk, built on the site of an old beacon.

In that part of East Sussex, there are many stories and legends current about "honest Jack Fuller", but the fact is that he seems to have been genuinely interested in science and music, for "he founded the Fullerian professorships, which he called his two legitimate children, and contributed liberally to the Royal Institution; and his musical parties in London were famous". One tale relates that when he grew dissatisfied with the Brightling choir, he presented the church with nine bassoons! The temple in that Downland Park is said to have been used for gambling, while the Sugar-Loaf, a pointed erection like a grey candle-snuffer set in the fields, is supposed to be linked with a bet that is worth recording.

The story goes that while away from home, 'honest Jack' boasted that the view from the lawn of his Rose Hill home included the top of Dallington church spire. When a guest denied this, a large wager was laid. Fuller returned home, only to find he was wrong. Hastily, he summoned masons to build an imitation of the top of the spire which could then be seen from his lawn on the skyline. So he won the bet! Pitt offered him a peerage, but he declined, saying: "I was born Jack Fuller, and Jack Fuller I'll die". Follow the road by the great wall of beeches just inside Brightling Park, and, less than a mile from the obelisk, you can stand by Jack Fuller's grave in Brightling church-yard. It is a large, depressing pyramid covered with moss and ivy. According to one authority, it was blocked up over sixty years ago. Another East Sussex legend of those parts states that Jack Fuller was buried "sitting up in an armchair fully dressed, with a church-warden pipe and a glass of port beside him". In Brightling church there is a bust of this unusual man. The inscription reads: *Utile nihil quod honestum!* The bet incident would seem to make a mockery of these Latin words.

From Beachy Head, you can travel westwards along the Downs to Cuckmere Haven, and also west of Newhaven, where Downland still persists, though not so spectacularly. East of Hastings we find cliffs again, and many stretches of sandy beach, sheltered from northerly winds. Even in historic times, the East Sussex coast has not been as stable as one would wish. Rye and Winchelsea were both medieval ports. Not only Rye but Winchelsea now stand inland, while parts of the western extremeties of coastline have sunk, mainly in the 13th and early 14th centuries, when much land was lost. The long, beauti-ful East Sussex coastline has many delightful seaside towns, from the large resorts of Brighton, Hove, Eastbourne, Bexhill and Hastings, to little estuary towns like ancient Rye.

Backed by the rolling Downs, they, together with the glorious country areas inland, are a paradise for painters.

Hollington Church-in-the-Wood, one of the smallest churches in the country, can be seen at St. Leonards on Sea, set in the heart of some 1,000 acres of rolling farmland and wooded valleys on the north-western slopes of Hastings. There may have been a church building at Hollington long before the Norman Conquest in 1066, though no sure evidence can be given. However, the chapel of Hol-lington did exist by 1090, and there was a Vicar there in 1291, though his name is not known. William de Mortkelene was the first Vicar (1302) whose name has been preserved.

Sometime during these last two dates, the Chapel of Hollington developed into a parish church with its own Vicar. In 1344, John de Leveryngton, Vicar of Hollington, left for another benefice, being replaced on September 26, 1344, by Robert Brok.

For a long time, certainly since 1742, the Church-in-the-Wood was believed to have been dedicated to St. Leonard, but evidence has accumulated since 1897 onwards to show that the original dedica-tion was probably to St. Rumbold. After the ancient Church of St. Leonard near the sea became a ruin around 1410, the people of that parish used the Hollington church. This may account for the

Fisherman's church and net shops, Rock-o-Nore, Hastings.

exchange of saints, St. Rumbold making way for St. Leonard as a mark of ecclesiastical courtesy. It was not till 1834 that a new Church of St. Leonard was consecrated by the sea front.

The church bell at Hollington is one of the fifty or so oldest in Sussex, and the only bell of such antiquity in Hastings. It was probably the work of William Burford, who died at the end of the 14th century. The beam across the nave in a building that claims no architectural distinction, is the sole survivor of the ancient timbers, a very large part of the church having been reconstructed at various dates between 1845 and 1934.

When the Church-in-the-Wood was built, a very large part of East Sussex was dense woodland, so it was natural that it would be built on a forest clearing, a fairly central position for the parish of those ancient times. The small, scattered parishioners would make their way to worship by footpath or bridle-track from many directions. Today, its situation seems peculiar, but was convenient then.

The church registers date from 1636, and the east window is interesting, being Belgian. Made in 1873 by J.B. Capronnier of Brussels, it was given in memory of Sir Charles Montolieu Lamb, Bart., of "Beauport", who died in 1860 and was the founder and Grand Prior of the Order of St. John. Notable descriptions of visits to the church were written (1823-26) by essayist Charles Lamb, and his poet friend Thomas Hood. What is of interest is, of course, the town expansion scheme. This is the development of the western side of Hollington into an overspill for 15,000 people from London. The Church-in-the-Wood will be in a strategic spot in relation to many of these new residents, and, obviously, there will be many changes in the parish.

From the sylvan beauty of Hollington, you can travel swiftly along the coast road and inland to ancient Rye, one of the Cinque Ports Confederation, that venerable group which guarded the gateway of England throughout the Middle Ages. From the time of Alfred the Great it has provided ships for the Navy, and it is thus entitled to guardianship of the western end of Romney Marsh, standing, as it does, on a sandstone rock at the end of a forest ridge.

G.K. Chesterton described Rye as "the wonderful inland island, crowned with a town as with a citadel, like a hill in a medieval picture". This impression persists today, for the picturesque assembly of inns, shops, houses, hilly streets and fortifications, rising to the apex of the 12th-century church, has not changed visually since Van Dyck drew it in the 19th century.

It is salutary to reflect that Rye's tourist trade employs, directly, or indirectly, more of the town's population than any other one industry. Despite sea recession, the rivers still enable Rye to provide wharfage for an assortment of craft. Boat building and maintenance continue unabated, and Mr. Phillips' Boat Yard, now in operation for over eighty years, is one of three Sussex establishments still building the Sussex lugger.

Romans, Saxons, Danes and Normans all, in turn, came to Rye. Known in Domesday Book as Rieberge, the present name is probably a corruption of *At ther Eye*, meaning "on the island". Rye was conferred on the Abbey of Fecamp by Edward the Confessor, and later, in the time of Henry III, reclaimed and made one of the Cinque Ports, being described, together with Winchelsea, as an 'ancient' town.

In those days it was not a peaceful place, being constantly attacked, plundered and sometimes burned by the French. Of its original walls, only fragments, together with the massive Land Gate, remain. Ypres Tower or Castle was one of the less successful fortifications against the marauding French. This stands on a cliff which, before the river silted up, overlooked the sea. Built about 1250, part of the fortifications are now used as the Town Museum. Incidentally, the two-mile walk along the quay at Rye to the Channel's edge is most rewarding, while any happy wanderer would feel great delight strolling along the sands to Camber for a day's exercise.

The timbered buildings in Watchbell Street are a visual delight. The town bell used to hang in Watchbell Street. Rye is a place of narrow passages and quaint houses. The former give unexpected and lovely glimpses of a town which can truly be described as unspoiled. Out of the holiday season, one can wander around the uncrowded street, and imagine it as it was in days gone by, when Rye was fully sea-side and the click-clack of mallets in the boat-houses was even more audible than in these ever-noisier times.

The town has a number of literary associations. It was selected as the ideal place by two American writers, novelist Henry James and the poet Conrad Aiken, whose daughters Jane Aiken Hodge and Joan Aiken are present-day Sussex novelists. Yet another American, Stephen Crane, author of *"The Red Badge of Courage"*, lived for a time at nearby Brede Place. The contemporary writer, John Burke, was born in Rye.

The parish church of St. Mary the Virgin, c.1150 to c.1300, is large and very lovely. Ranging in styles from Norman to Perpendicular, its most famous architectural feature is the carved altar of the St. Nicholas' chapel. The old clock, the "Vinegar" and "Breeches" Bibles, the bells, with inscriptions, the fine windows, one by Burne-

Jones, whose windows also grace St. Margaret's Church, Rottingdean, and the tomb of tragically murdered Allen Grebell, an 18th-century Mayor, are all of interest. Incidentally, there is another feature, sometimes missed — a cistern (reservoir), built of brick in 1735 and now in the churchyard. Reduced to a ruin in 1377, the church was rebuilt between 1400 and 1500. It has been described as "the goodliest edifice of its kind in Kent or Sussex, the cathedrals excepted".

One of the finest architectural features of a place packed with interest is the Old Grammar School (1636), the nearby *George*, the Landgate gateway (one of three built around 1380) and the Augustine Friday (c.1380), commonly known as The Monastery, and now used for commercial purposes. Then, there are the 15th-century Old Hospital reconstructed in the next century, the Town Hall (1742) packed with its lovely silver regalia and treasures of past centuries far too numerous to list, the Old Stone House, built around 1263 and a survivor of the great fire in 1377 which almost burnt the town to the ground, Lamb House, probably rebuilt in the early 18th century, but with evidences on the site of a late 15th-century house, and the notable *Old Flushing Inn*.

Without doubt, the most famous part of Rye, with its endless cobbled streets and timber-framed buildings in contrasting styles, is the steep Mermaid Street with famous Mermaid Inn, a former Smugglers' haunt. All other considerations aside, Rye and The Mermaid go together like the 'horse and carriage'. This fantastic hostelry is a main jewel in the town's crown, something of which Ryers, the people of Rye, are justifiably proud. Situated on a one in three gradient, it has a medieval air, with original black oak everywhere, the wood carvings smoothed down by centuries of feasting and festivity, a hostelry without peer in the realm, impossible to copy, a truly great English inn in East Sussex. There have been some changes, of course, and only in 1956 did it get a full licence which enabled people to drink without dining. One suite is called 'The Hawkhurst', after the notorious gang of smugglers who were linked with the Kent village of that name. There is also an elegant bedroom named after the fictitious Dr. Syn, and a four-poster suite called 'The Elizabethan Chamber'. Such a brief survey does inadequate justice, but in retrospect, it makes one long to return for further hilly rambles of discovery.

Finally, let us not forget the countless attractive shops, such as Dewe's Apothecary Shop in the High Street, and the wares of Rye Pottery in Ferry Road. This has contributed to the potting traditions of Sussex for over 100 years, first at the Cadborough works. Exam-

The clock on Rye church.

ples of Cadborough and Rye potteries, plus decorative moulds used in the last century, are on show in Rye Museum.

Today, after more than five hundred years of civic work by its townspeople, the former borough of Rye has been amalgamated since April, 1974 with the surrounding rural district and Bexhill to form what is now Rother District Council. Rye remains a parish in the new District, and will retain important powers and duties.

Before leaving this absorbing part of the far East Sussex coastline, let us make a little trip inland to Udimore and Winchelsea, then wander over to the historic town of Hastings and the modern seaside resort called Bexhill-on-Sea, with a shingle beach. On the way, for good measure, we shall call at Pett, Brede and Fairlight.

Udimore stands on the main road from Rye to Brede (B2089), a village that straggles around and boasts a place-name of Cock Marling. The church stands away from the village, and is so close to a big farm that it seems as if one of the old out-buildings is intruding into the graveyard! Originally planned for another site, there is a legend about the church. The first plan, said authority, would be too low, and lead to possible inundation. Every night, stones built up during the day were scattered by unseen hands, while 'supernatural' voices chanted "O'er the mere! O'er the mere!". Finally, the builders obeyed, and moved to higher ground. Now, the name Udimore is supposed to derive from "O'er the mere". Those who consider it ridiculous should reflect on peculiarities of dialect, especially that *th* is pronounced *d*.

I like the notion that Udimore is a village where one can expect a long life. There is a tablet in the church which states this: *Death will come at last. To the Memory of Widow Marshall, late of this parish, who died the 9th March 1798 Aged 98 years".*

A Second World War story is linked with a shop in Udimore where business was carried on for many years by a family called Field. A report appeared in the 'Sussex Express' about a wartime crash of a Messerschmitt 109, shot down by British fighters. The heading said "VILLAGE SHOPKEEPER CAPTURES GERMAN PILOT". This referred to Mr. Eric A. Field, a special constable, who had served in the First World War, and knew the ropes regarding prisoners. The report read:

"Shot down by British fighters, a Messerschmitt 109 crashed in a south-east village last week. The proprietor of a local stores walked up to the German airman, who was uninjured, and took him prisoner, keeping him locked up in his shop until the arrival of Army officers. This shopkeeper now treasures a receipt which, to put it mildly, is rather unusual, for it announces the 'receipt' of one German pilot".

Like Rye, the town with which it is always linked, Winchelsea has little love for the French. Those 14th- and 15th-century raids were dreadful events, and it is certain that the little town nearly perished from both the French and the sea. Once situated at shore level, it was all but swept away in the 13th century. Petitions for help were sent to Edward I, but nearly fifty years elapsed before the King's Treasurer and the Lord Mayor of London came to East Sussex to have a look for themselves. It was only then that rebuilding was agreed, and this took place on the high plateau where Winchelsea stands today, something which, surely, makes Edward I the first of the town planners!

It was at Winchelsea, described by John Evelyn as "all in rubbish, and few despicable hovels and cottages only standing" and by one poet, un-named, as "a town in a trance, a sunny dream of centuries ago", that Edward III commanded his fleet against the Spanish, who gathered together off Dungeness and fought their way into Rye Bay. His Queen, Phillippa, is reputed to have watched the battle, at some distance, from Udimore. If there is a question mark connected with this event, what about the ghostly sound at Winchelsea of the horses of highwaymen, executed in 1782?

Queen Elizabeth called it 'Little London' because of its industry and loyalty, John Wesley preached under an oak tree near the New Inn, and Franciscan Friars lived there from the 13th century, traces of them still lingering today.

Three of the town's old gates remain, one being rebuilt five hundred years ago. In olden times, there were thirty-nine squares. Today, the only remaining one is round the church. Grey Friars, all that is left of a 14th-century monastery, is now the finest house in the town, and faces the old harbour. Splendid to see is the long-ruined windmill one of the best-known landmarks in the country. After losing its sails in two mighty gales it was reduced to a sad spectacle. Dating from the 18th century, it has a round-house at its base on which the mill rests. This is reached by a tall flight of stairs. The round-house has now been re-roofed. The mill itself was built in 1760, but early last century it was carried two hundred yards to where it now stands, all without being dismantled!

Finally, there is the parish church of St. Thomas, which possesses some fine canopied tombs, Crusaders' tombs, and the monument of Gervase Alard, Admiral of the Cinque Ports in the latter part of the 13the century, claimed to be "the best in all Sussex".

2

AROUND THE VILLAGES

Pett lies inland south-west of Winchelsea, and is greatly admired for its commanding position. The church, rebuilt in the 1860's, has a tower that can be seen for miles around, but tops a sombre church which still commemorates George Theobald, who, in 1641, gave a handsome gift to it.

> "He gave a bell freely to grace the new steeple,
> Ring out his prayse therefore, ye good people."

Along Pett Level, the beach tends to build up against the sea. Once visitors depart, however, birds swoop down from the skies to take over the scene again, and it can suddenly become quite lonely and oppressive.

At the turn of the 19th century, two eccentric brothers, Daniel and Edward Thurston, lived in a little tumbledown shack on the foreshore of the small hamlet at Pett Level, near Hastings. Old and peculiar, they travelled around by pony and trap, mending leather bellows. They also went the rounds of outlying cottages in the marshes between Pett Level and Rye, including the *Old Ship Inn,* which once stood on Winchelsea Beach, whose landlord had the old marshland name of Cooke. Considered 'odd' by the locals, the brothers were shunned, and the shack became known as 'Uncle Tom's Cabin'. Made from an old boat, it had a little fireplace and living quarters built from driftwood, and the two old men lived there in what any self-respecting person would regard as smelly discomfort. They supplemented their income with a flourishing trade in fish, shell fish and shrimps, which are plentiful off the shore at Cliff End. They also kept a few sheep on the free marshland. An amusing tale about them is related by Keith Cowper in the September, 1973, issue of "*Sussex Life*". It appears they would not pay their bills for hay and feed. "Once, when cornered by the local farmers in their 'cabin', one of the Thurstons tore a patch from his old jacket, put it in his pipe

34

and lit up. The resultant smell was enough to put their creditors to flight".

Icklesham is a pretty and rewarding place. From it, one can branch across to Brede, almost due north from Westfield, with which it has links. Let us wander through Icklesham first. Here, again, there is a windmill on its horizon facing the sea, a high Norman tower built in tiers and packed full of arches and windows, and one of the best Norman naves in East Sussex, indeed in the county. In Icklesham church there is an unusually complete sequence of Early to Late Norman architectural features. Massive pillars have beautifully carved capitals, each one different. Above these are corbels holding up a modern roof, the work of 19th-century masons, whose oak leaves, vines and roses are surely the work of the font makers. Apart from the porch, Icklesham church is barely changed from the 13th century.

At Westfield there used to be a manor house where Lankhurst Farm is today. By the 19th century, this beautiful house had passed to the Frewen family through marriage. One member, Stephen Frewen, a son of Puritan John Frewen of Northiam, was an Alderman of the City of London, and lived at another manor house, nearby Brickwall. Today, the Frewens still live at Brede Place. which is open to the public every summer. Although originally built in the 14th century, it was altered in the 16th century, Tudor bricks being used, after which it remained unchanged. Treasure-stocked Brede Place contains many mementoes of former famous visitors, including many peices of scupture by Clare Sheridan. She once owned the house, and bronzes still there include busts of Lenin, Trotsky, Zinoviev and Kamenev, produced when she visited Russia as early as 1920.

E.V. Lucas once had this to say about the old manor: "This house, like all the old mansions (it is of the 15th and 16th centuries), is set in a hollow and is sufficiently gloomy in appearance and surroundings to lend colour to the rumours that would have it haunted . . . " He was, of course, thinking not of a priest who is said to haunt the house, but of an early Oxenbridge, of whom there are some in the church, who was an "ogre and dined of babies". No one could kill the monster with ordinary weapons such as bows and arrows, so he was eventually sawn in half with a specially-built wooden saw. The place where this blood-curdling act occurred is called Groaning Bridge. Brede was once the haunt of smugglers, who used the house as their headquarters.

During October 1830, recorded as a wild and storm-swept month,

Sailing at Piddinghoe.

the poor peasantry of Sussex along the Kent border, where there had been disturbances, suddenly erupted into violence. The East Sussex night skies glowed with the flames of burning ricks. Most gentry and land-owners became mortally afraid for their lives and possessions, being suddenly surrounded by utter lawlessness. The rural poor, bitter about their dire conditions blazed with wrath in what was England's last Peasants' Revolt.

One of the major causes of discontent was the introduction of machinery, especially threshing-machines. They blamed their squalid conditions on these "inventions of the Devil". Many were unemployed, while those doing work received an average weekly pittance of between 7s.(35p) and 8s.(40p). "The threshing-machines would have to go", they said, "and their wages raised by 2s.(10p) a week."

After an October of blazing ricks, the first really serious event did not take place till 4th November, when a protest meeting was held at Brede. The next day, four chosen farm labourers negotiated with eight farmers and a minister at a meeting held in the *Red Lion Hotel*. Their main grievance is recorded as being against the activities of a Mr. Abell, assistant overseer of the local workhouse. The following resolutions were adopted:-

> "The gentlemen agree to give every able-bodied labourer with wife and two children 2s.4d. per day from this day (5th November) to the 1st of March next, and from the 1st of March to the 1st of October 2s.6d. per day, and to have 1s.3d. per week with three children, and so on according to their family.
>
> "The poor are determined to take the present overseer, Mr. Abell, out of the parish to an adjoining parish and to use him with civility."

It is satisfying to read that the detested Abell was civilly pushed out of the parish in the parish cart, and, probably uncivilly, dumped across the boundary by gleeful labourers who were first applauded by local farmers, then treated to a mug of ale.

Tempers ran so high that troops had to be sent to Battle. Labourers gathered there sent a message to more at Sedlescombe. They, with other adjoining labourers, were invited to join in resisting the military. This, in fact, did not happen, but the troops' appearance at Battle resulted in further uprisings in other parts of East Sussex. Rotherfield, Ringmer, and Lewes were involved, but only events like those at Brede occurred. The activities moved to perimeter villages

Mayfield village sign.

of the Ashdown Forest. Wage riots took place at Buxted, Mayfield, Crowborough and other villages.

While all this was going on, a secondary aim of East Sussex farmers was the reduction of tithe charges to help them pay the increased wages demanded of them by their poor labourers. At Dallington, a village near Battle that possesses one of the few stone spires in the county, the rate-payers sent a letter to Sir Robert Peel, part of which reads almost like a national and financial lament of the present day. ". . .that altho' unable to bear it we have met the wishes of the magistrates in this district by RAISING THE WAGES OF THE LABOURERS AND THE RELIEF OF THE PAUPERS on a scale which we positively cannot continue for any length of time without bringing us all to one common ruin, and which we have done to prevent our property from being destroyed by incendiaries."

During the Peasants' Revolt, fifty-two cases were brought to trial in Sussex. One man was executed, sixteen were jailed and seventeen transported to Tasmania. Some wage agreements were kept, many were not. Improvements did not become evident for another 20 years. By the time living conditions were tolerable, the 1830 uprising had become a fiery entry on the pages of the East Sussex history.

Tucked away among fairly flat, lush countryside, lies Beckley, dotted today with a mixture of imposing new and renovated old houses. A few boast the possession of an oast house, a reminder of Kent's proximity. Much of Beckley is pure sylvan delight. The war memorial stands at the end of its main street, together with the 14th-century church encircled by Spanish chestnuts. Pause for a while in these peaceful surroundings and admire the church's lychgate, which has St. George and St. Michael under canopies, the fine windows, many 15th-century with their multitude of colourful saints, and much admirable wood and iron craftsmanship typical of East Sussex.

At one time, the present Duke of Bedford's parents lived in The Place House, Peasmarsh, near Rye. William Pattison, "the Chatterton of Sussex", was born in this delightful village in 1706. He died of smallpox at 21, and wrote satires, epigrams and odes in imitation of Pope, Bird, Waller and Gay, and was befriended by bookseller Curll. The ancient church of Peasmarsh, rather remote in a park, was restyled in the 14th century, and again later. By the chancel arch are two peculiar lions in red sand-stone, one biting his tail. It is recorded that one of the tower bells, dated 1631, is inscribed "Hatch made me".

While in that area, track across the Rother valley to Bodiam Castle, nestling almost like a bird on its watery moat, which, some consider, "wins more respect than if it had stood a siege". Built in the 14th century by Sir Edward Dalyngrydge, it is now a romantic ruin in fair preservation. The place itself is steeped in history which finds much expression in the church. This has a curiously shaped tower with a corner turret, and the bells were peeled for the first time in 1761 in farewell to a parson who preached innumerable sermons there. Bodiam hops are also noteworthy, and are used for a well-advertised and famous brew! Those acquainted with Sussex speech have assured me that Northiam is not pronounced by the natives as it is spelt. *Norgem* is its local style, just as Bodiam is *Bodgem* and Udiham is *Udgem*. However one pronounces the name, the local villager is quietly proud of the place, and, to prove it, has this couplet:-

> O rare Northiam, thou dost far exceed
> Beckley, Peasmarsh, Udimore and Brede.

Having seen them all, I cannot accept this judgment as absolute, though parts of it are sound. For instance, although Northiam cannot boast a Brede Place, nor its name match that of Udimore, yet Northiam alone possesses Queen Elizabeth's Oak, the tree beneath which the great monarch partook of a banquet in 1573 whilst on her way to Rye. The fare was brought from the kitchen of the nearby timbered house of a Master Bishop. During her visit, Good Queen Bess changed her shoes, and the discarded pair is still treasured at Brickwall, the neighbouring seat of the Frewens, the great Northiam family for generations. Made of green damask silk, the shoes have pointed toes and heels two-and-a-half inches high. The first Elizabeth was, it seems, so well satisfied with her proudly-presented repast that on her return journey three days later, she dined again under the same oak tree. It is not recorded that she changed her shoes on that occasion!

At Burwash traces of a Cistercian Abbey remain on the river bank. A memento of this is housed in the Bodleian Library, in the shape of an old volume containing the inscription: "This book belongs to St. Mary of Robertsbridge; whoever shall steal or sell it, let him be Anathema Maranatha." Since nothing more tangible than a chain ever protected books in those days, the volume did pass into other hands, and this is written under the original inscription: "I John Bishop of Exeter know not where the aforesaid house is; nor did I steal this book, but acquired it in a lawful way". When the Abbey of Robertsbridge was suppressed by Henry VIII the lands passed to Sir William Sidney, grandfather of Sir Philip. At Abbey Farm are a 13th-century arch in the wall of the farmhouse, the double crypt below the farm-

View of Rye from the church tower.

house floor, and fragments of the abbey walls. Some of its tiles are in the British Museum, and there is a stone in Lewes Museum, found on the farm in 1823, which is a remnant of the handsome sculptured figure of Sir Edward Dalyngrydge, the 14th-century hero builder of Bodiam, whose remains rest in the abbey on the banks of the Rother.

Salehurst, regarded as one parish with Robertsbridge, (where Malcolm Muggeridge lives in Park Cottage, which countless admirers hope will be preserved as a museum eventually), claims as its distinction the fact that the remains of the founder of the Pelhams, a name encountered all over Sussex, and the family name of the Earls of Chichester, rest there. It was he who captured the King of France at Poitiers, and was granted permission to include the royal Buckle in the Pelham badge. Here, in the abbey at Salehurst, Sir John Pelham chose to lie. There can be little doubt that his wife's remains lie there also, and it was she who defended Pevensey Castle during a siege while her husband was away.

A mile or two north-west of Salehurst is an ecclesiastical treasure, the oldest dated brass in Sussex, set in the chancel floor of the 14th-century Church of the Assumption of St. Mary and St. Nicholas at Etchingham. It depicts Sir William de Echyngham, who built the once-moated church in Decorated style between 1360 and 1380. The founder, alas, has been headless since 1788, and his brass is one of six fine ones in a building that is extremely high in proportion to its length and breadth. The nave seems very short in comparison with the long chancel, and some consider it likely that it was originally planned on a larger scale. Above the impressive east window mullions are shields of the Plantagenets, John, Duke of Brittany, son-in-law of Edward II, Edward III, John of Gaunt, and Edward, the Black Prince, who defeated the Spaniards off Winchelsea in 1360.

Sir William's brass has a Norman-French inscription which says:

> Of earth I was made and formed
> And to earth I have returned.

The rather squat tower, topped by the original copper weather-vane which represents the Echyngham Arms in the shape of an inverted banner, has one bell dated 1632, and inscribed "John Wilmer made me". According to local legend, an earlier bell fell into the moat, and "may be recovered from its watery grave by six white oxen". To the left of the south door is an interesting plaque to Sir Henry Corbould, whose body lies in the churchyard. He was a friend of the renowned painter, Chantrey, and is remembered as the designer of the Penny Black postage stamp. The plaque, which is carved in his likeness, is the only known representation of Corbould, who is said to have died in neighbouring Calehurst of apoplexy. Many believe he was buried by the then vicar, Hugh Totty, who began 66 years of preaching at the Etchingham church in 1792.

From Etchingham, we will back-track through Ticehurst with its medieval Bell Inn and 13th-century St. Mary's Church with stone faces and gargoyles that have been brooding above the churchyard for 700 years, and Wadhurst, high on the forest ridges and possessing a set of unique Iron Age tombstones, deriving from workers at the time when the last fire in a Sussex iron furnace was put out at Wadhurst. This is an area crammed with historic villages far too numerous to detail, but simply asking for investigation. However, of most interest is 12th-century ruined Bayham Abbey, a place of beauty and tranquillity far removed from the glitter of the East Sussex seaside resorts.

Standing in a blissful setting on the bank of the little River Teise,

Bayham Abbey is only just in East Sussex, being on the verge of the Sussex-Kent border, some two miles from Bella Yew Green, near Frant. Standing some 600 feet above the sea, Frant has a lovely green surrounded by wonderful scenery, and a 15th-century church, refashioned in the 19th century, with a tower from which one can see the cliffs at Folkstone.

Originally known as Begeham Abbey, Bayham was built as a priory in honour of St. Mary, and was the abode of the White Canons, members of the Premonstratensian Order, instituted around 1120 at Premontre, France. Many Sackvilles were buried there, having contributed large endowments. Other sums were granted by several Charters from King John, Henry III and Edward II. Unfortunately, Bayham Abbey was among the first to be dissolved by Cardinal Wolsey. The value of the priory was recorded as £152 19s.4d., regarded at the time as a large sum.

Today, the ruins indicate the former vast extent of the building, also its beauty, and one can sit and reflect at leisure by the fishpond, just as the monks did 700 years ago. It is a spiritual experience not to be missed. It is also a comforting thought that much patience and skill have been shown in the abbey's restoration by the Department of Environment's Inspectors of Ancient Monuments.

3

BATTLE AND HASTINGS

Moving south-east again, via Brightling Beacon, whose Needle, staning 646 feet high, is sometimes shrouded in a sea of mist, we come suddenly on Penhurst while making haste to Battle Abbey, *Le Souvenir Normande*, which, half a mile to the south, was the scene of the Battle of Hastings on 14th October, 1066 on nearby Telham Hill, where, history reports, a "hoary apple tree" grew in Harold's day.

First, pause at Penhurst, a former centre of the East Sussex iron industry, where high above Ashburnham Park, a lonely 15th-century church stands by a farmhouse of the same period. St. Michael's Church has screen tracery that may be 14th century, a Perpendicular west tower, box pews with doors, and a Jacobean pulpit and reader's desk, with the customary stumpy blank arches. Nearby Court Farmhouse is reputed to be 17th century. Three-quarters of a mile west stands brick-built Court Lodge, early to mid-17th century. Ashburnham Furnace, near this mullioned-and-transomed-windowed house, was the last iron smelting works in Sussex, and was still busy in 1813, or thereabouts. The advent of modernity and motor transport seems, as yet, to have made little impact on the peace of the place.

Penhurst and Ashburnham are permanently linked, the manor of the former having been absorbed a great number of years ago by the enormous Ashburnham estate. Down the hill stands the Ashburnham forge, a mysterious, immensely quiet reminder of the Iron Age. It is said there are too many ghosts around here to be counted! One fact beyond dispute is that the famous Sussex firebacks were a feature of the Ashburnham forge, mere bagatelles compared with the cannon-balls and cannon on the railings of St. Paul's Cathedral which were produced there.

This little town of Battle, whose name reeks of the fierce slaughtering that took place in 11th-century East Sussex, speaks of the even deeper fact that the Battle of Hastings is the most important conflict of English history. It is likely that the ancient town would never have

Sycamore tree growing through workshop roof in Russell Crescent, Brighton.

existed but for that mighty massacre by the Normans. The reason is simple. Battle Abbey emerged from the conflict; the town developed as a result of the Abbey. The relationship between abbey gatehouse, where one enters, and town market place still proves the point.

How did Battle itself derive its name? It springs from the Conqueror's vow, made while preparing for the Battle of Hastings at Senlac, and recorded in great detail in Lower's translation of *The Chronicle of Battle Abbey*, around 1180. "... I make a Vow, that upon this place of battle I will found a suitable Monastery, for the salvation of you all and especially for those who fall ... "

Such an enterprise demanded workpeople. They formed the nucleus of the first town, which still nestles close to the *Ecclesia Sancti Marini de Bello*, as early Royal Charters of William and succeeding Norman kings of England named the "Abbey of St. Martin of Battell."

It was Bellum in the charters, La Batailye in the 11th century, Batayle in the 14th century, Bataill in the 15th century, Battell in the 16th century, Battel in the 17th and 18th centuries, and now, Battle, which has been its name since those labourers turned the first sod.

What of the town's growth to its present population of around 31,910? It is true to say there has never been any undue growth, for so conservative were the successive lay owners of the Abbey estates in their devotion to Battle that as recently as 1924 the number of private holdings in the town was almost exactly the same as recorded in 'The Chronicle of Battel Abbey', around 1100, that is 115.

It is only since 1924 that new housing has appeared along nearly all the approach roads into the town, leaving its centre much as it has always been. A 17th-century inhabitant of Battle, if he could return to the town today, would have little difficulty in finding his way from, say, the 'crooked house' in Mount Street, or the windmill on Caldbec Hill, to the Parish Church, and indeed would see much that was very familiar to him. What growth there has been, has been slow by modern standards. In 1150 the population of Battle must have been between 750 and 1000. By 1750 it had probably risen to 1500. By 1801, the first census year and when Battle's barracks were full of troops for the Napoleonic Wars, it was 2040. By 1851, when the railway was being built, it was 3849, including 600 railway labourers. By 1901, 2996; by 1921, 2891; by 1931, at the start of the expansion period after 1924, it was 3491, rising by 1961 to 4517. Thus in the last 200 years Battle has grown in population from 1500 to 4517.

True to the vow he made, William the Conqueror ordered work to begin quickly on the Abbey of St. Martin, Bishop of Rome, who was martyred by the Emperor Heraclius in 655. Standing in a circle of nine miles, containing vineyards, dew ponds and rich land, the building itself was quadrangular. Just outside was a small street of artisan's dwellings, where all things needed by the monks were made. The church was the largest in the country, larger even than Canterbury. It was also a sanctuary, any sentenced criminal who managed to shelter in it receiving absolution from the Abbot, the first being appointed in 1076.

William did not live to see it completed, and William Rufus presided over the consecration in February, 1095, a ceremony recorded as "of great grandeur". Sixty monks of the Order of St. Benedict came to Battle from the Abbey of Marmontier in Normandy to form its nucleus. William Rufus presented his father's coronation robe and the sword he had wielded in battle to the abbey, to which several wealthy manors were attached and the surrounding country exempted from taxation. The Abbots were made superior to episcopal control, and endowed with the right to sit in Parliament, with a London house to live in during the session. Nothing, in short, was left undone that could minister to the power and pride of the new abbey.

In 1200, King John "was there, shaking like a quicksand. He brought a piece of our Lord's sepulchre, which had been wrested from Palestine by Richard Coeur de Lion, and laid it with tremulous hands on the altar, hoping that the magnificence of the gift might close Heaven's eyes towards sins of his own. In 1212 he was at Battle Abbey again, and for the last time in 1213, seeking, maybe, to find in these silent cloisters some forgetfulness of the mutterings of hate and scorn that everywhere followed him."

Other kings went to Battle Abbey. Henry III galloped up to its gates just before the Battle of Lewes. Accompanied by a brutish crowd of horsemen, he levied large sums of money to help him with his struggle. After the battle, still greedy, he returned as an exhausted refugee.

A very different story is recorded about the welcome visit of Edward II, who slept there on the night of 28th August, 1324. The then Abbot, Alan de Ketbury, went to great lengths to show hospitality. His contribution to the kitchen included "twenty score and four loaves, two swans, two rabbits, three fessantes, and a dozen capon; William de Echingham sent three peacocks, twelve bream, six muttons, and other delicacies; and Robert Acheland four rabbits, six swans, and three herons."

In 1331, a group of French maurauders were kept at bay by Abbot

Blacksmith's forge at Glynde.

Hamo and his monks. The intruders had landed at Rye, and were halted at Battle Abbey until the country gentlemen were able to assemble and drive them away. Two peaceful centuries followed, but then came disaster of a different kind in 1538. In order to examine the state of the Abbey, Thomas Cromwell sent down two commissioners to report its condition back to the "zealous Defender of the Faith". The two commissioners found "nineteen books in the library, and rumours of monkish debauchery within the walls". One of the officers wrote: "So beggary a house I never see". The Abbey was suppressed, and presented to Sir Anthony Browne, upon whom the "Curse of Cowdray" was pronounced by the last departing monk.

If genuinely pronounced in those far-off times, the curse has certainly been terribly fulfilled. When Sir Anthony Browne, father of the first Queen Elizabeth's host and friend when she stayed at Cowdray House, seized his new property, turning the monks out of the gate in 1538, it is said that the last monk warned the despoiler that his line should "perish by fire and water". This came to pass very quickly. A week after Cowdray House was burnt, in 1793, the last Viscount Montagu, was drowned in the Rhine. His only sister, wife of Mr. Stephen Poyntz, who inherited the estate, was the other of two sons, both of whom were drowned while bathing at Bognor. When Mr. Poyntz sold the estate to the Earl of Egmont, the curse seems to have been withdrawn.

Among the many treasures destroyed in the fire were fine paintings and the Roll of Battle Abbey. A few years before its demolition, Doctor Johnson visited Cowdray. "Sir," he said to Boswell, "I should like to stay here four-and-twenty hours. We see here how our ancestors lived!".

Nothing now remains of the refectory, where some forty monks ate together in contemplative mood. Only the walls stand, devoid of the former noble roof of Irish oak, taken to Cowdray to perish there with the Abbey Roll.

Such events seem far removed from the Battle of today. Like other places of great antiquity, it is gradually easing its way into modern living. One can only reflect that those gory "battles long ago" probably paved the way for the vigorous, forward-looking Battle of today.

To all who know, and love the ancient place, Hastings and the greedy sea are indivisible. It was the sea that brought the Danes, who have left more marks on Sussex as a whole than is often realised. What about the gentle memorial of King Canute's daughter under the raven tile in Bosham Church in West Sussex, or the evidence of names like the Wicks, The Hoove or the Hasting, all to be found

Hastings Castle.

along the coastline where tideway or creek give sanctuary to the long boats?

The sea, of course, won its last battle over resistant land at Hastings. It made England an island, independent of France and the Continent. It was also, remember, at Hastings that the Norman conqueror was brought by sea, landed on our chalky shores, vanquished the Saxons, and thus made England politically dependent on France and united to the rest of the Continent's mainland, a *volte face* indeed! History, in fact, wrote itself in letters of blood when it came to the pages of East Sussex.

Stepping firmly into the present day from those ancient times, one finds much on the East Sussex coast that creates dismay — things that have aroused watchfulness on the part of various hard-working preservation societies. In Hastings, it is advisable to look for the sign *'To the Old Town'*. There, the true main street greets the eye, with its stepped pavement and rows of ancient, slightly tipsy houses still in fine shape. The street curves round to the foot of the eastern cliffs and the fishermen's area, known as The Stade, an old Saxon word meaning "landing place". It is situated at Rock-o-Nore, meaning 'the rock against the north', and for most people the short stretch of coast from Bourne Road to east of Rock-o-Nore is the most attractive feature of historic Hastings. Some consider it par excellence along England's southern coastline, except, perhaps, in the west country.

Stand on the eastern breakwater and, to the left, see the fleet of

View of Lewes from the Castle walls.

Hasting luggers and fishing vessels drawn up on the beach as, beloved by artists, they have been for centuries. This is probably the only fleet now left in England that is drawn up on the beach. Move along east of the fishing vessels and you find the Net Shops, even more sought after by painters and poets. Unique in our land, they draw residents and visitors alike to stand, gaze and admire — even, sometimes, to have a chat with a bearded, keen-eyed 'salt', busy mending his damaged nets.

Certainly Elizabethan, and probably of earlier origin, they are reduced to around 43 from 109 standing about ninety years ago. In 1936, the capstans, one to each trawler and previously operated by horses, were replaced by motor winches. East Well, a spring at the foot of East Cliff, which had supplied the fishing fleet with fresh water for centuries, was in 1760 described as "Excellent for Making Tea". It was also used as the 'East Well' address for the area until 1859, when the name Rock-o-Nore was substituted. The Fishermen's Church was built in 1854, and was in use till 1939, when services stopped. During the Second World War, it was occupied by the Army and Home Guard as a rest billet. Subsequently, it became a commercial store until 1956, which was resented by the fishermen, then it was reconditioned, to their relief, from a near-derelict state, and became the Fishermen's Museum in the same year that marked the completion of the present fishmarket. Two other noteworthy buildings in the area are East Cliff House, built by Edward Capel, Censor of Plays, in 1761, and visited by the great actor, David Garrick, and Lavendar House, built in 1789 when the brick tax was in force (1784-1850), and fronted with black glazed vitrified tiles. Until 1957, Hastings was saddened by the deterioration of her Net Shops. Their extinction seemed inevitable. Then, a miracle happened. Funds were available from the Museum Barrel Fund. It was agreed that the shops could be saved if work began at once. Mainly, the work has resulted in new concrete bases and considerable new weather-boarding and tarring. By 1959 no fewer than 23 had been repaired and restored. Some were shifted to new bases to make room for a footpath on the south side of Rock-o-Nore Road.

The old fishing quarter also boasted the original Bo-Peep Inn, once a favourite rendezvous of smugglers, and indicated on a local map as being sited in adjacent St. Leonards-on-Sea. The unusual name is said to derive from the lines in the nursery rhyme:-

"Let them alone and they'll come home,
Bringing their tails behind them."

The first part was obviously a warning to the Preventives, as the Excise men were known, and the "tails" were the kegs slung across the ponies' backs. Stirring East Sussex days, by any standards.

In June 1961, five shops were destroyed by fire and two others were blown down in a gale. This great disaster was beyond the repair means available from the Barrel Fund. No appeal was made, but the disaster was reported in the "*Hastings Observer*" and on the Museum notice board. A footnote asked for any donations to be sent to the Midland Bank in Robertson Street. The immediate response was astounding. In the first month, £1,000 was donated. This enabled work to start right away, and proved the public's affection for these unique buildings, and its desire for their preservation. A plaque commemorating both fire and restoration was unveiled by the then mayor of Hastings, Councillor Douglas William Wilshin, on Easter Monday, 1961.

The Old Town still possesses much of its quaint yester-year charm. It nestles snugly in the valley between East and West Hills, and is the premier Cinque Port. However, for all its proud history as a port, the harbour silted up, and the decline began.

There was little change until Georgian times. Then, when the fashionable world began to flock to Brighthelmstone, soon changed to Brighton, some doctors, notably a Doctor Baillie of London, discovered that Hastings air was a "Sovereign remedy" for chest complaints. From then on, the Old Town turned with enthusiasm to a new career, destined to become one of this country's most attractive and popular resorts.

In December, 1975, it was reported that a new look is to be given to the Hastings Old Town Hall Museum of Local History under a joint scheme by the Area Museum Service for South Eastern England and Hastings Borough Council. Ground Floor displays will cover the prehistoric to medieval periods, with sections on the Battle of Hastings and the Augustinian Priory. Upstairs sections will illustrate different aspects of Historic Hastings, such as law and order, trade and commerce, architecture, tourism, travel, the church, the sea and the Cinque Ports and pastimes. Over 20,000 visitors went to the Museum during the summer of 1975. When finally arranged, the displays should become a magnet for tourists in the South-East.

Apart from its fabulous historic background, modern Hastings is crammed with interest, holiday facilities and entertainment of all kinds, including the delightful Stables Theatre.

St. Mary-in-the-Castle is a most unusual church, classical, semi-circular and possessing a running stream in one corner. The ruins of

53

Keere Street, Lewes.

Norman Hastings Castle top West Hill, its dungeons having amazing acoustic properties. Noted St. Clement's Caves, once a smugglers' haunt, the walk from East Hill to lovely Ecclesbourne and Fairlight Glens, and the romantic Lovers' Seat, are all now part of an extensive country park covering over 500 acres, stretching over four miles and affording unsurpassed panoramic views of the Channel and Sussex coastline.

Every May, the Blessing of the Sea Rogationtide ceremony is held in the fishermen's quarter. In contrast, the Hastings Embroidery can be seen in the Embroidery Hall at the White Rock Pavilion. Commissioned in 1966 to commemorate the 900th centenary of the Battle of Hastings, the 243 ft. long embroidery was made by hand at the Royal School of Needlework, and records in vivid colours, 81 of the great events in British history since 1066. Less romantic, but equally vital, an expanding light industrial output now helps the economic life of the town, and is largely contained within the Ponswood Estate, much as Brighton's light industrial life is found at Hollingbury on its northern perimeter.

The renowned archaeologist, John W. Moore, lives in Hastings, and is known for his work at the internationally famous site of Star Carr, Yorkshire, and other sites from Neolithic to Saxon times in the same county. Some of his most recent excavations in East Sussex have been on the Belgic site at Fairlight and Cliff End, Pett, where 8,000 years ago survivors of hunting traditions of the Mesolithic period left some meagre finds as their cult was waning. At that time, the marshes in the region extended across to the European mainland, and archaeological links have not been resumed until 2500

Southover Grange, Lewes.

B.C. Near Fairlight Church, some of Britain's first Neolithic farmers found patches of light soil for emmer wheat cultivation. They were descended from the last European hunters who had later mingled with the new farmers and learned their trade.

Next came the Belgae, or Iron Age men, from the Continent, who left a curious record at Fairlight quarry. Their huge, timbered, thatched and whitewash-daubed barns were the ones Roman historians mentioned. Until recently, the floor of such a barn was visible. John W. Moore excavated the greater part of it at the southern end, but it has now been filled in. There have also been Romano-British finds west of Fairlight Glen, where a hearth held pottery fragments of Roman style, yet imitated in native British pastes. This was also a feature of the Fairlight quarry finds, where local people obviously imitated Belgic wares.

From 50 B.C. during the Belgic domination of Kent and parts of Sussex, until 200 A.D., when the Romans' military rule crushed the Celtic spirit, the invaders' wares were imitated in soft, earthy, less durable terms. Some authorities think they were made by the women-folk of those remote times as part of their domestic chores, but it is an assumption which, so far, has not been proved.

Hastings was the birthplace of the distinguished author Malcolm Saville, whose famous children's books, of which he has written about sixty, have at least four set in Rye. His grandfather, the Rev. Alfred Thomas Saville, a former LMS missionary in the South Sea Islands, was a minister at Rye for 27 years before moving to Hailsham, after his wife's death, and preached his last sermon in the market town's Congregational Church. He died at St. Leonards-on-Sea in November, 1915, two of his children, the Rev. W.J.V. Saville and Dr. Lillie Saville, RRC, following him into the mission field.

Malcolm Saville's first Sussex book was "*Gay Dolphin Adventure*", set in East Sussex in his beloved Rye.

One serio-comic note about Hastings must be its famous Winkle Club whose call to action "Winkle up!" is a universal phrase which, seventy years ago, would only have signified inside the limited confines of the Old Town's fishing community. How greatly this has changed is illustrated by the following story. When in the 1966 General Election, the late Richard Dimbleby was announcing the results during the night following polling day, he came to the Hastings figures. Looking up with a wide grin, he greeted his fellow-Winklers. It is safe to assume that quite a good proportion of his vast audience appreciated the point of his greeting.

Hastings Winkle Club was founded in 1900 in one of the fishermen's favourite Old Town "locals", the Prince Albert. Now defunct, that event has guaranteed its immortality. Money-raising was its object, begun in the days before the Welfare State, dispensing good cheer at Christmas to the children of those working-class familites who often, especially in winter, lived in conditions bordering on poverty.

Seeking a suitable emblem, the story goes that at the first memorable meeting, providence caused someone to turn up with a pail of winkles. That did it! From then on, every member must carry a winkle, whose original occupants have been removed and replaced by sealing wax, and failure to do so at meetings means a fine, much more now than the penny demanded in those early days! The Queen, as Princess Elizabeth received a gold Winkle Brooch on 18th May, 1951, and Sir Winston Churchill was presented with his on 7th September, 1955.

If Brighton can lay claim to Friese-Green for cinematography, Hastings is proud of the fact that John Logie Baird started his researches into television in what is now a shop in Hastings Arcade, on which a plaque records the fact. There is also one to his memory on a house where he once lived in Bexhill-on-Sea, a very sick man who, like many other British inventors, made nothing out of his creative genius.

The town is also linked with the famous (or infamous) Lady Hester Lucy Stanhope, daughter of the Earl of Stanhope, whose ideas about politics and science were far ahead of his time. Born on 12th March, 1776, at Chevening in Kent, she once tried, while in Hastings, to escape from her governesses and row over to France. It is recorded that she was summarily brought back to the town and thrashed! In 1806, her uncle, William Pitt the Younger, left her a pension of £1,500 a year, a fortune in those days. On 10th February, 1810 she sailed for the Middle East in the frigate "Jason", and never again set foot on her native soil. Years later she became the acknowledged Queen of the Arabs! — an event that fulfilled a prophecy made to her by an astrologer named Brothers.

Not only is Hastings concerned with the past, it has the future very much in its sights. One sporting event alone proves this, the International Rugby Festivals. Over the past years, the Festival has attracted clubs from Sweden, Belgium, France, Italy and the United States, and has aroused a great deal of interest in the international Rugby world.

CASTLES, CHURCHES,
AND CONTRABAND

One reason why chroniclers think William the Conqueror's army moved to the east may have been the sight of a forbidding landmark, the Roman-Saxon fortress of Pevensey Castle, obviously strongly defended, though ruinous, and quite prepared to trample on any who dared invasion. There is no doubt that the Pevensey area was the scene of repeated medieval attacks. Extensive excavations, made many years ago by the Sussex Archaeological Society, unearthed relics of pottery and coins that prove the fact beyond argument.

One of the earliest places to be fortified by the Romans, the present walls of the town are believed to date from around 250 or 300, at least. They offer most interesting evidence of the thorough way in which the Roman legions consolidated their victories. The walls are built on a clay bed 15 feet wide, anchored by driving in oak stakes. On this was laid a footing of clay and flints, some three feet deep, and then massive timbers with an over-lay of nine inches of concrete. The wall was then built on this intricate foundation. It was 12 feet 3 inches thick, 28 feet high, and made of greensand blocks, filled in with a rubble core. Inside each wall was piled a clay bank about 4 feet 6 inches above the plinth, an engineering feat that would receive respect today. It is easy to imagine those stirring times just by studying the nine massive bastions, or towers, along the walls. Main defence points, they were built to outlive the centuries, solidly constructed of cemented flints and cased with stone. This fortress, known as *Anderida* was one of the stations subject to the authority of the "Count of the Saxon Shore". Shortly before the Norman Conquest it was raided twice by Earl Godwin and his sons, in 1042 and 1049.

After William's victory, Pevensey was given to his half-brother, Robert of Mortmain, who built a stone keep, now in ruins. Two hundred years later, Peter of Savoy lived there and built other fortifications. The next four sieges, between 1066 and 1400, were undertaken

Entrance to Glynde Place.

* * *

by William Rufus, 1088; Stephen, 1144; Simon de Montfort, 1265; and the supporters of Robert of York. Then it fell into decay for some centuries, and what remains has been presented to the nation by the Duke of Devonshire. Under National Trust guidance, it is preserved in its present state for all time.

*   *   *

Bodiam Castle, on the north-east line of the Kent border past Robertsbridge, has just about the widest moat possible, huge, round battlemented towers at its corners, square central towers linked by weighty walls, and a general appearance of ageless immensity. In some ways it looks, from a distance, like a huge sandcastle on the beach.

Those menacing towers rise about 60 feet, and the walls about 42 feet. The great portcullis over the Great Gate has 13 iron points, and is surmounted by four ancient coats of arms. There is even an echoing dungeon, the Lady's Bower and the Great Chamber, a room some 50 by 18 feet, where the knight, Sir Edward Dalyngrydge, who built Bodiam Castle in 1368, probably presided at table, and discussed Poitiers and Crecy as we, today, might talk about the Battle of Britain, June 1940, or the Normandy landings in 1945. Bodiam Castle, now a romantic ruin with a wide, deep moat which looks idyllic when the waterlilies are in bloom, was saved from destruction and given to the nation by Lord Curzon. Sir Edward Dalyngrydge built the castle 180 feet square with walls six feet thick. One of its most impressive features is the twin-towered gatehouse, with tops built outwards to provide shutes through which molten lead could be poured down on any intruders! Sir Edward's personal history deserves more space than this brief account allows, but mention must be made of the pathetic echo of the past, a battered stone in Lewes Castle once sculpted to represent the famous man of the Hundred Years War.

*   *   *

Hastings Castle is a Norman structure that instantly creates an awesome sense of time. Sometimes, it seems as though little has happened at Hastings Castle since Leonard Mascall of Plumpton, further west, with its late Bronze Age settlement on nearby Plumpton Plain, first introduced carp to the moat around the Tudor House associated with Lutyenes and rare birds. The occasion is recorded in these lines:-

> Hops and turkeys, carp and beer
> Came into England in one year.

As the sea made Sussex, so is it always the county's enemy and potential destroyer. In distant ages, East Sussex man could walk from Brighton to Boulogne, just as the other side could cross from Calais to Dover. Rollers from the Atlantic chewed their way up the English Channel. North Sea waves rubbed out some of the Straits of Dover. At last, the two waters met head on, and Britain became an island. One Sussex geologist maintains that the East Sussex part of the county stood out longest against the double sea attack. The last land-bridge, or isthus, that joined England to France was made of the Wealden rocks of Hastings, whose Castle, built by Robert, Count of Eu shortly after 1069, is now half-down in the sea, lost as surely as William the Conqueror's sword was lost in the destruction of Cowdray Castle. Close by, at Bulverhyth, is a massive block of stone. Its claim to a place in history is the reputed fact that the Conqueror dined on it. As yet, it has not been swallowed up.

In those far-off days, time was always of greater value to the smaller and more passionate forces deployed. The inefficiency of the weaponry and projectiles made refuge in a strong fortress vital, and Hastings Castle was such a place. The shape of the hill it dominates was just right for fortification in the Dark and Middle Ages. It could cover a landing or repel an invasion. It could protect the large and ever-increasing population. In its best form it is comparable with Chateau Gaillard in Normandy, and, to a lesser degree, with Lewes, also Arundel to the west. In short, a kind of peninsula, or spur, with a lofty summit, united with hills to the rear by a narrowish neck, over which assault would be impossible.

Under modern conditions, these arrangements are bad, but in the 11th and early 12th centuries they were ideal. When the Conqueror held Hastings there were no projectiles strong enough to be thrown at the castle from the hills to the north-east. By the time of the third Crusade, some hundred years later, such weapons had been invented. Stand, surrounded by its history, on the platform of Hasting's ruined stronghold, and realise that, for at least the first hundred years after 1066, the place must have been quite impregnable. Suitably, it had the epithet "ceaster" attached to it in Anglo-Saxon times. This was never given to any place that had not been properly fortified, either by the Romans or their successors.

*   *   *

With delight I turn to the sheer poetry of Herstmonceux Castle, the home of the Royal Greenwich Observatory since 1948, when it moved from Greenwich because of too much disturbance. For this, a number of new buildings emerged, none worthy of comment except the equatorial group, completed in 1958, east of the castle. This is a group of six silvery domes for equatorially mounted telescopes, and one feels a strange kind of excitement when glimpsing them for the first time, shining like incredible beehives in the surrounding formally-laid landscape, thick with trees. The present Director of the Royal Greenwich Observatory, which celebrated its tercentenary in

The newly restored Dacre tomb at Herstmonceux Church.

1975, is Dr. Alan Hunter, who was awarded a C.B.E. in the 1975 Queen's Birthday Honours List.

The three northernmost domes are designed for reflector instruments. This meant planning that allowed for interconnection, and easy access for instruments through trap-doors for re-silvering. The other three are for refractor instruments. Each dome has a balcony, used when watching for approaching clouds. Their bases are on concrete and brick, the domes themselves being of steel and copper. In tune with younger architectural thought, the details are refined and elegant rather than robust.

This modern interpolation only adds to the splendour of Herstmonceux Castle itself, once Hurst Monceaux. By any standards, it is a fairy-tale sight, a dream of moated beauty, with soft red brick blending superbly with lush greenery. Without doubt, it is the finest brick-built castle in Britain, and in some ways, beyond true description. It has to be seen to be believed. The mere fact it is of brick is noteworthy. Although the material appeared throughout the Middle Ages, it only became fashionable when Herstmonceux appeared, examples of like kind in other counties being Tattershall in Lincolnshire, Caister in Norfolk and Faulkbourne in Essex.

A magnificent legacy from the 15th century, Herstmonceux was built by Roger Fiennes, who became Lord Dacre. When completed, there was no brick structure to equal Herstmonceux in the country, with its four courts and walls 200 feet square. Today, as through the centuries, it is one of the major architectural gems of the south of

Southease Bridge.

England, with its astounding windows, its dark moat still encircling the walls, round towers 84 feet high, and the great gateway, one of the noblest in the land. The castle itself is unfortunately generally closed to visitors.

In 1777, Herstmonceux Castle was owned by Robert Hare, a Canon of Winchester, whose second wife managed to persuade him to demolish it and build Herstmonceux Place out of the materials. She tried to prevent Francis Hare-Naylor, her step-son, from inheriting in favour of her own children, but the land and property entailed could not be diverted, and her off-spring did not inherit the place.

Francis, a friend of Charles James Fox, eloped with Georgina Shipley, younger daughter of the Bishop of Asaph. They lived in Italy for a time, and she became a pupil of the Greek scholar and one of the few women professors of the age, Clotilda Tamboni. Of their four sons, Augustus Hare, the diarist, related the family story in his *Memorials of a Quiet Life*. Another became rector of Herstmonceux, whose curate was John Stirling, friend of Carlyle.

From all accounts, Georgina was renowed for her eccentricity in Sussex, and Italy. Seated, white-robed, on a white ass, she was accompanied when she went to church by a white doe which sat on the end of her pew. She often visited Weimar, where she became a friend of Goethe and Schiller while attending the Court of the Grand Duchess. "Full of faith, hope and resignation", she died in 1806 at Lausanne. In 1829, a monument by the Danish sculptor, Kessels, pupil of Bertel Thorwaladsen, was placed in Herstmonceux Church. The length of time between her death and the erection of the monument was simply due to the fact that the first one was lost at sea, and the family ordered another from the same sculptor. After her death, Francis Hare-Naylor sold the place, and it remained a ruin until it was restored by Colonel Claude Lowther, lord of the manor until 1929.

The 16th-century Dacre tomb, restored in 1970 at the wish of Mrs. Elizabeth Dacre, is well worth a visit. A tablet in memory of Air Commodore Dacre has also been placed in Herstmonceux church. A local master mason, Mr. George Elliot, was responsible for the complicated restoration of the Gothic monument erected in 1534 in All Saints Church, Herstmonceux, to the memory of Thomas Fiennes, second Baron Dacre of the South (1490-1533), and his son, who predeceased him, Sir Thomas Fiennes (1490-1528), from which line Air Commodore Dacre was descended.

Lord Dacre was kept a prisoner in the Tower of London by Henry VIII, and later beheaded. His lands were restored to Sir Thomas

The village of Ripe.

when Elizabeth I came to the throne. When restoration work started early in 1970, the full-size stone effigies of two men in armour had damaged and broken feet. The arches of the ornate canopy, with its beautiful heraldic devices, required painstaking refurbishing to bring them back to their present glory. Advice on heraldic matters was given by Mr. C.W. Scott-Giles, OBE, FSA, FHS, Fitzalan Pursuivant Extraordinary. The memorial tablet sculptor was Mr. Kenneth Eager. The well known architect, Mr. John Denman, also assisted.

Situated between the North Chapel and the chancel, the tomb consists of three different types of stone, namely, Purbeck marble, Caen stone, some of which can be seen at St. Margaret's Church, Rottingdean, and Bonchurch stone. The table tomb chest is Late Gothic, decorated on both sides with panels of four quatrefoils, cusped and sub-cusped, each separated by narrow 'doll's head' motifs. The two effigies are superbly carved in Caen Stone, their facial aspect being wonderfully life-like. They are dressed in Milanese armour of about 1490, their heads rest on Brocas helms, and their hands are in the attitude of prayer.

It is believed these effigies reached Herstmonceux as part of job lots disposed of at Battle Abbey after the 16th century Dissolution of the Monasteries.

The Dacre title, non-existent for hundreds of years, is now held by Baroness Dacre, a member of the House of Lords, and wife of playwright William Douglas-Home.

*   *   *

The Lewes area, now the seat of local government for East Sussex County Council, is notable for the massive preservation and restoration that has helped retain some of the county's finest architecture. Lewes Castle, surveying the proud admixture of modernity and the Middle Ages huddling at its feet, was founded by William the Conqueror's son-in-law, William de Warenne, and was first built of flint, not wood, about 1100.

In Southover Church, near Lewes, the mortal remains of William de Warenne and his wife, Gundrada, the Conqueror's fifth daughter, are buried in a small modern chapel, built in Norman style. Two small lead coffins rest under two arches. By them is a lead casket, and there is a remarkable stone, engraved in black marble, in the middle of the floor.

Digressing from Lewes Castle for a moment, it is interesting to record how this church, the Priory of St. Pancras, came into being. When William and Gundrada travelled to Rome around 1075, they visited, en route, the majestic abbey house of the Cluniac order, then reaching the peak of its authority and fame. The Pope of the time was Gregory VII, also a Cluniac. William decided to introduce the Cluniac reforms to England, and in 1077 gave a brotherhood of Cluniac monks a small church at Southover, south of Lewes on flat land. A larger stone church must have been begun at once. It was consecrated first before 1098, the internment of Gundrada being in 1085 and William de Warenne in 1088. The site of the 11th-century church has been revealed by excavations, many of them by the Lewes Archaeological Group.

Lewes Castle is a truly noble edifice to view, either from a distance, or from the ancient, narrow street that weaves its timorous way through the great gateway of the mighty two-bastioned barbican, one of the most splendid in England. For me this bastion somehow expresses the personality of the first de Warenne, who held his East Sussex kingdom "By God and by my sword".

A succession of de Warennes extended the structure, including the old town walls, of which only a portion remains today. For some old Lewes residents this is a cause of constant regret. If those old walls were intact now, I was told, they would "keep out all these foreigners". This speaks much for ancient Lewes and its pride in isolation. Other East Sussex centres welcome visitors of all kinds not only for their interest but their revenue. Not so the stiff-necked East Sussex county town, which rightly cherishes its traditions along with its brooding, turreted castle. There, with the ruined walls, remains a tunnel-vault, north of the keep, which belongs to a house along the path west of Castle Banks, and some chalk masonry of a mound which was called Brack Mount. Incidentally, the keep is a shell-keep, inside which is a Serlian doorway with moulded bands at intervals. There are also some Gothic windows dating from the time when the keep was used for the more pleasant purposes of a summer house.

*   *   *

When the Conqueror and his men landed at Pevensey Bay in 1066, the first landmark they must have glimpsed was the Church of St. Peter, founded in 774 by Offa, King of Mercia and overlord of the South Saxons, and standing on a hill in what is now Bexhill Old Town. From it, a wide view includes what used to be Downland to the sea, and to the south-west, where Hooe Level leans against Norman's Bay, Cooden, originally Cooding, has emerged on a shore where a submerged forest originally broke the low tide water.

To the west, also clearly visible, the fortress of Pevensey, though ruinous, was obviously well defended, and may have been one reason why the Norman forces went east, undoubtedly careering through the ancient thoroughfares of High Street and Church Street, in what was then called Bixlea, as they made for Standard Hill, their marshalling point to the north. They probably passed the old forge, now an antique shop, and manor house, now ruined on a

Charleston Manor, West Dean.

site overlooking the sea, which William gave to the Norman baron, Count of Eu, who is also recorded in the Domesday Book as owning the Manor of Herste, now Herstmonceux.

In that semi historic survey, Bexhill was granted a place, while nearby Hastings was only mentioned as part of the reference. Its importance only declined when its landing facilities and shipping shelter proved less adequate than those of Rye, Winchelsea and Hastings. In good weather, vessels used to beach sideways, unload and float off on the next high tide. Supplies were carried over the undeveloped shore to the hilltop town up Sea Road, then called Sea Lane.

With these conditions, smuggling was rife. It was also regarded as a "respectable occupation", and some Old Town residents still boast about their great-great-grandfathers' exploits. Old account books at Sammy Pocock's butcher's shop in High Street, established in 1801, show some strange entries which have nothing to do with the meat trade.

There are still some old families in Bexhill, notably the Mittens, the Rogers and the Llewellyns. Nearby Park Cottage has been lived in continuously by the Rogers, well-known builders for some 170 years. Linkwell, the Llewellyns' home on the south side of High Street, facing across to Beachy Head, the Belle Tout Lighthouse and the famous Seven Sisters cliffs, is the Old Town's most famous example of Regency architecture. The architect is unknown, and the colonnaded front elevation is rarely seen, being turned away from the road. Possessed of an early Georgian 'servants' wing, Linkwell was the site of two of the many wells on the Old Town's hill-top, one being the Town Well with a public entrance from High Street.

The people of Bexhill are proud, both of its ancient traditions and the fact that it has the De La Warr Pavilion, one of the most elegant theatres in England, completed in 1935.

Before sweeping inland again, where we find names like Jevington and Friston, away from the resort atmosphere, let us move westwards to Eastbourne via East Dean and Birling Gap beloved of smugglers like, for instance, Jevington Jigg. At one time, he operated in the Cuckmere valley, running the contraband in the Birling Gap, then to a farm at Friston called Crowlink, and thence, by Cuckmere's banks, to his own village and beyond. At Jevington lived a very co-operative clergyman, whose cellars, though bursting with plunder, were always able to accommodate a few more kegs. Jevington church is called St. Andrew's, patron saint of seamen (so who shall question his governance of smugglers, too). In the church are two strange objects. One is a memorial tablet showing the date of

1694, which provides for the new as well as the old calendar. The other is a stone relief, considered Saxon, showing, so local worthies have it, Christ thrusting a staff into the Serpent's head.

Almost all Sussex was involved in this illicit business over the centuries. In a literary connection, even Alexander Pope was not above profiting by it in 1717! Both land and sea smugglers were needed for getting wool out of England for sale to French and Flemish merchants. Gentry were often involved in smuggling wines, spirits, tea and silk. Even the occasional local parson was not above such nefarious pursuits! Pevensey Bay was also much used in this way in the 18th century, and Burwash lay right on the smugglers' inland communications line. There, the Bell Inn was a favourite calling place for the 'Gentlemen', while Bateman's, Kiplings famous home, was once a smugglers' headquarters. There is a tradition that smugglers used a vault for illicit storage beneath one of the tombstones in Burwash churchyard. Carved with a repulsive skull and crossbones, it topped an underground passage running towards Bateman's, the old ironmaster's house which now belongs to the nation, and is dated 1634 on a stone over the door. It seems certain that this local tradition inspired Kipling's weird "*A Smuggler's Song*", which is concluded by these lines:-

> Five and twenty ponies,
> Trotting through the dark —
> Brandy for the Parson
> 'Baccy for the Clerk

Them that asks no questions isn't told a lie —
Watch the wall, my darling, while the Gentlemen go by!

Whipping Post House at Rottingdean, to the west, was once the home of the ancient village's famous smuggler, Captain Dunk. It has now been so restored as to have virtually been rebuilt, but, sad to relate, it now bears little resemblance to its former historic appearance. Only one good thing can be said about it. The site of the old village whipping post, used for the chatisement of "scolds and the like", is marked by an original chestnut tree, left standing on the grass patch beside the house.

Finally, not many people are aware that there is a smuggler's hideout under what used to be Mockford's greengrocer's shop in Rottingdean High Street. This takes the form of a gloomy cavern, from which a tunnel probably still runs down to the beach.

5

EASTBOURNE AND
THE SOUTH DOWNS

If Bexhill has the De La Warr Pavilion, Eastbourne has its fine Congress Theatre, the grandest of Grand Hotels in the country, the fine Towner Art Gallery, a massive influx of annual visitors, and a population of some 70,000 residents. Reputedly not steeped in antiquity, though this is untrue, its main claims to fame range from a most equable climate and diversity of attractions to the majesty of Beachy Head and, westwards from that dizzy height, the chalky, turf-topped Seven Sisters, standing stolidly with their feet in the swirling sea. The name Beachy has nothing to do with the beach. It is probably derived from the Normans' description, "beau chef". The Seven Sisters start at Birling Gap and extend westwards nearly to Seaford.

It is a pity that Eastbourne suffers from misunderstanding about its historical value. Its rapid growth has led to the misconception that it was without any history or importance in bygone days. This is not true. The geology and prehistory of the district, the occupation of what is now Eastbourne in Celtic times, its importance under Roman rule, and its final settlement by a large Saxon population, to whom many place-names are owed, and whose organisation and field system survived the Norman Conquest, are all aspects that have, in the main, survived to present times.

In the Middle Ages, when it was an aggregation of townships whose chief occupation was agriculture, manorial records show a considerable population, the ample proportions of the parish chuch confirming this fact. What has mitigated against discovery until quite recently is Eastbourne's geographical position. With the South Downs to the west and a wide space of rich marshland, in earlier times open water, to the east, it had few, if any, important highways. Again, to the north lay the great forest of *Andredsweald*, extending right across Sussex. This produced considerable isolation, and it was not till 1780 that Eastbourne came to the notice of royalty. Then, the three younger children of George III, with tutors and governesses,

Strange rock formations below the tideline at Beachy Head.

arrived in the town "for the sea-bathing and other advantages that the place offered". They did not stay in the Old Town, where some antiquity might have been found, but at sea front "sea-houses", the visit lasting over four months. In August 1804, an appreciative notice was published which stated that "in spite of the menace of the enemy, this little watering-place has to boast of the fullest season ever known".

Again, in August, 1824, the then vicar, Dr. Brodie, wrote to a friend:- "Eastbourne is as full as it can well hold and very respectable; we had more gentlemen's carriages at church last Sunday than I have seen for many years, and the church so crowded that many were obliged to leave for want of seats". Finally, a Guide Book to the place was published as long ago as 1787, combining in prose and verse, a descriptive account of "the various beautiful prospects and diversified scenes of this healthy and romantic spot." Such a description justifies the equally glowing comment made about Eastbourne by the late Godfrey Winn in his book "*This Fair Country*". When young, the former writer, who lived at The Mill House, Falmer, in the last years of his life, and died on 19th June, 1971, while playing tennis in its grounds, stayed in a Marine Parade boarding house run by a Mrs. Chandler. After retiring one night, he had this to say about the view from his bedroom: "When I reached my little front room at the top of the house, I threw open the window, and leant far out, and for a moment, the sweep of the bay with the coloured lanterns might have been the Promenade des Anglais at Nice".

In 1975 former pupils of Moira House School, founded in January 1875, and operative in Eastbourne from 1888, descended on Eastbourne from all parts of the world for its centenary celebrations. Probably one of the least publicised of our "progressive" schools, its contribution to the improvement of women's education has granted it a unique place of significance in the history of education. Chiefly distinguished through its contributions to the performing arts, the BBC's first religious drama series was adapted from a Moira House production, "At the Well of Bethlehem", written by former principal, Mona Swann.

Eastbourne College is a distinguished boys' public school in a town long associated with education.

Promenade, Eastbourne.

Eastbourne, of course, has considerably tamed Rudyard Kipling's "Whaleback Downs" from the sea inland to Polegate, with its tower windmill of 1817 to the south, of which the four sails survive, and an early 14th-century chapel at Ottenham Court. It belonged to a grange of the Premonstratensians, founded in the late 12th century, and soon afterwards coming under the jurisdiction of Bayham Abbey, now the most impressive monastic ruin in the country, and situated on the Sussex-Kent border south-east of Tunbridge Wells.

East Dean is to Eastbourne what Kingston is to Lewes or, say, Ditchling is to Brighton. Earthworks and tumuli prove that this valley had ancient settlers. The Saxon tribe of Beorl is reputed to have given its name to the manor that became Birling. The church at East Dean has a stalwart Saxon tower, though the interior lacks supporting monuments with which one tends to associate antiquity. One old stone commemorates the Bardolf family, busy in the 13th and 14th centuries. An 18th-century wall tablet, one of two in the chancel, is to 'Nicholas Willard, gent.', probably a descendant of an earlier Nicholas, churchwarden of Arlington around 1685. The East Dean family resided at nearby Crowlink, so were probably concerned, with the Jevington Jigg smuggling. Earlier still, a priest called Henry Wyllerd is referred to in a document dated in Henry VIII's time. He seems to have been connected with church matters at Friston, and had a name which seems exclusive to this part of East Sussex.

*   *   *

The South Downs stretch right across East Sussex from the Western side of Eastbourne, and part of the area bordering on Friston Forest to the north, plus a section of the Cuckmere valley and a portion of the famous Seven Sisters Country Park. Acquired by East Sussex County Council in 1971, with the aid of an Exchequer grant, it is recognised as a Country Park by the Countryside Commission. During 1972, the Council's countryside committee outlined a number of objectives for which part management should aim in a lush area, with unique features in the south of England, which lies within the Heritage coast stretching from Eastbourne to Seaford. These include one of the few undeveloped river estuaries in the region, and a large part of one of its last remaining stretches of unspoilt cliff scenery. It is a place of wonderful solitude, with an unusual variety of plant and bird life, and with a literary history, geological features and landforms of outstanding interest. The County Council is now striving to conserve these features as being important for the well-being of people who live in the crowded south-east. When fully preserved, the Seven Sisters Country Park will prove a superb gem in the crown of East Sussex. The Exceat farm buildings have been converted for car parking, and there is a horse-riding track from Exceat, once a flourishing village but now non-existent, to New Barn, and back via Foxhole. From Exceat Hill there is a lovely view of the silvery Cuckmere, whimsically curving its journey to the sea. The village declined after being struck by the Black Death in the middle of the 14th century, was later ransacked by French raiders, and by 1460 there were only two houses standing in the village on the eastern shore.

Moving along hedge-flanked roads a little to the east, one finds Charleston Manor, mentioned in Domesday Book, and now the home of Lady (Rhoda) Birley, artist widow of the renowned artist, Sir Oswald Birley. Apart from the house, the annual Charleston Manor Arts Festivals are also a delight to attend. Walter Godfrey, a great expert on ancient buildings and monuments, especially in Sussex, assessed the oldest part of the house at around 1080-1100, and the Romanesque window probably dates from around 1100 to the beginning of 1200. Tradition has it that the Conqueror's Cup Bearer and his mother lived in the early part of the house, though this has not been conclusively confirmed. However, the fact that a Cup Bearer and his mother lived there is indubitable. Walter Godfrey affirms that she ordered a church to be built there, but in her will demanded that it be pulled down after her death as she feared sacrilege. He also considers there was a Saxon building on the site before the Norman period. Lady Birley's first festival was in the Royal Pavilion at Brighton, which she rented for a fortnight, using a great deal of the original furniture graciously lent by the Royal Family in 1946. After the third Brighton Arts Festival, she started to hold her Charleston Festival partly in the Royal Pavilion and partly at Charleston Manor. After this, she started giving horticultural lectures in the 16th-century tithe barn, one of the finest in the county, but then fast becoming a ruin. It was finally restored by Lady Birley's sale of their London house and studio, together with donations from the Historic Buildings Council and East Sussex County Council. The first Charleston Manor Festival was held in its present form in 1968, great help being given throughout by Miss Doreen Pugh. It is said that Alfred the Great had a royal home at West Dean, where Asser the monk visited by appointment, later becoming a Bishop and Alfred's biographer. Above West Dean, with which Exceat was merged, and which, in turn, is now one with Litlington, pine is worked with beech.

Southease Church, showing round tower.

Although pine trees are somewhat alien to Sussex, there is a heady quality along the broad, grassy avenues that span Friston Forest. Hilaire Belloc, in fact, said that when he smelt pine trees he breathed Sussex air, a viewpoint open to debate. Litlington Church has traces of a rood loft and a twisted, leaning spire, a wooden shingle one with a weatherboarded tower. There is a Tudor west window set in the flintstone wall and, unexpectedly, Norman work within. Incidentally, Litlington's tiny village claims to have poineered the tea-garden movement in Sussex. Set on a gentle slope down to the Cuck-mere, it has not only the oldest tea-garden in East Sussex but in the county. History also records that a former Rector of Litlington was not averse to the smuggling, 'Gentlemen' using his church for purposes quite unrelated to prayer. His reward, of course, was an occasional keg of good brandy.

Go slightly north-east and you reach the Benedictine priory at Wilmington, founded in 1050 by Herluin de Conteville, and part of the huge grant of the Rape of Pevensey made by the Conqueror to his half-brother, Robert de Mortain. He, in turn, gave Wilmington to the Abbot of Grestein in Normandy, as recorded in Domesday Book in 1086. Eventually the place fell into dissolution. A fine house was built in a part of the Priory buildings, and in the 16th century it was used as a vicarage for the nearby church. Later, everything became the property of the Sackvilles and was leased to Thomas Culpepper, another name of renown. He, together with his wife and nephew are buried in the church.

Like those of Michelham Priory, the Wilmington ruins are administered by Sussex Archaeological Society, and are open to the public. The upstairs rooms house an agricultural museum, not totally out of place in what was a farm for generations. The second museum room was the Prior's chapel. The Tudor kitchen is below. There is an underground vault from which, it is said, a passage leads half to Milton Street, a scene of cottages and farmsteads short of the Downs. It is almost certain that smuggling went on here, too. Like Tarring Neville, east of Alfriston, Milton Street seems to bask in perfect peace.

The mention of Alfriston makes me revert for a moment to smuggling and the Stanton Collins gang of cutlass, blunderbus and pistol-packed ruffians who took over Alfriston, and made the timbered Star Hotel, among the oldest in England, one of their resorts. It has a quaint carving of St. George and the dragon beneath a bow-window, and a strange, 400-year-old wooden lion figurehead from a shipwreck standing in a corner, almost like a smuggler's guardian. Stanton Collins used the Market Cross, now Ye Olde Smugglers' Inn, as his headquarters, and was eventually arrested and deported, not for smuggling but sheep-stealing!

East Sussex has many unusual trees, especially those sculpted by the often strong prevailing south-westerly winds. Wilmington churchyard lays claim to one of the most interesting yews in a county where the oak is one of the most familiar trees, being associated with the heavy Wealden clay but thriving best of all on rich, sandy loam. Crowhurst's immense yew has a bole 28 feet in girth and 5 feet from the ground. There is little doubt it was a very considerable tree when the battle of Hastings was fought not very far away. Another East Sussex veteran yew stands at Herstmonceux. A source of supply at one time for the vast numbers of long-bows needed even at Flodden in 1513, yews are generally regarded as emblems of immortality. As for tree sculpture, there are some fine examples in Lewes Crescent, Kemp Town, and in other parts of the county. For a curiosity, what could be more surprising than the sycamore tree growing through the roof of a building behind the Compton Arms public house in Dyke Road, Brighton?

Constant speculation about the incredible Wilmington yew tree is nothing compared with that surrounding Wilmington's Long Man, carved out of the north side of the Downs above the village. Experts are still baffled by it, a landmark for miles. Some have suggested it is, like the Cerne Abbas Giant in Dorset, of Bronze Age derivation, a survival of some primitive fertility cult, maybe even an 18th-century joke. Whatever else it is, it has justifiably been described as the "largest representation of the human form in the world". It was even tidied up at one time by members of the Eastbourne Christian Youth Council. In 1873 it was outlined in yellow bricks for greater permanence, and the present outline of white blocks, which visitors are specially asked not to walk over or on, was laid in 1969. The slope of the hillside provides an optical illusion of breadth instead of height. The lengths of the east and west staves are 230ft. 8ins and 235ft.8ins, the distance between them being just half their mean length. The figure is rather less, and well-proportioned.

On the way to lovely 13th-century Michelham Priory at Upper

The Long Man, Wilmington.

Fourteenth-century gatehouse at Michelham Priory.

Dicker, one can digress to the market town of Hailsham, which has a 15th-century church in the middle of a busy street. Note on the way the farm at Otham, with the chapel now used as a barn. Hailsham church stands on the ridge bordering Pevensey Level on the west. It is capped with pinnacles like those at East Grinstead to the north, and now in West Sussex, where we have the noteworthy Adeline Genee Theatre, opened on 29th January, 1967, and, despite vicissitudes, in its fourth year as a charity management.

Not far from Hailsham lies Polegate. Less than a century ago Polegate's only water supply came from a small brook flowing along the bottom of a strip of land about 30 yards wide.

Unfrequented by humans, the land was a paradise of wild-life, both flora and fauna, with upwards of 40 varieties of flowers, plants or trees, and foxes, rabbits, hedgehogs, moles, the occasional snake, butterflies, dragonflies and bumble bees. Probably the largest resident bird was the magpie, and while rooks, crows and heron kept clear, there were finches, wagtails, linnets, sparrows, thrushes and blackbirds. Now, with the exception of the Lombardy poplars, everything has been bulldozed away for housing.

Before leaving this area, it is advisable to see something of Hellingly, which is tucked away between two main roads, the A267 and A271. It has what is reputed to be the only intact round churchyard in Sussex. Note how the ancient form has been recognised by the building line, and what a fine crescent is made by the cottages facing inwards to the churchyard. As the reformed faith was practised at Hellingly, the minister was burned at Lewes in 1557.

Several manor houses abound. One, with the weird name of Horselunges, is a moated 14th-century building that belonged to the Deveishes. Hellingly Park takes us back to the Dacres of Hurstmonceux. While poaching deer from Sir Thomas Pelham, Thomas, Lord Dacre, killed a keeper. For this, the young Dacre and three fellow huntsmen were executed in 1541. The Cuckmere flows gently from Hellingly across lush countryside to Michelham, where it becomes lost in the moat.

HARTFIELD, CROWBOROUGH, WITHYHAM AND ROTHERFIELD

Before going to Michelham Priory, visit Hartfield, where 'Beggar-man Smith' lies in the churchyard. The story tells how some 300 years ago, Nicholas Smith, a rich man of Sussex, disguised himself as a tramp. Hartfield was the only place where he found kindness, so he remembered the village in his will, and his bounty is still distributed each Good Friday, at his graveside, by the rector and church-wardens, about 25 villagers each receiving 25 pence. Upper Parrock, home of the famous British film producer, Sir Michael Balcon, is mainly 15th century but partly 16th. The most recent restoration was in the thirties under the supervision of the well-known Sussex architect, the late Walter Godfrey.

Some records, it is said, speak of a one-time renowned iron *mistress*. Reliance was placed on the importation of European specialist labour, in conflict occasionally with the locals. Craters in the surrounding woodlands have been identified as the remains of iron workings. In the late 19th and early 20th centuries, yeoman farmers apparently occupied the house, signs of hop growing being evident. All farm buildings and oast houses were removed about 40 - 50 years ago.

From Hartfield to Crowborough is a delightful journey, with the latter standing at some 800 feet on the Forest Ridge, and possessing a cross-roads house where Richard Jeffries lived and wrote his last essay. On to Heathfield, standing in a valley painted by Turner, the picture being in the Tate Gallery. Heathfield House stands in its park, where the three-roomed Gibraltar Tower rises 55 feet. It is said that 40 churches can be seen through a telescope from its summit, and the naked eye can see from Beachy Head to Devil's Dyke. Its name commemorates Lord Heathfield's time as Governor of Gibraltar near the end of the 18th century. A more recent attraction is the Heathfield Wildlife Park, in which the Gibraltar Tower stands.

Within a stone's throw of Hartfield, Withyham is not only an East

South Downs Way, Ditchling.

Sussex jewel, but shines in the county's history. The nearby Ash-down Forest influence seems to enrich the air and promote a glor-ious feeling of well-being. This pretty village with its lovely church, excellent inn, the *Dorset Arms*, Duckings, a rich piece of old East Sussex architecture, and the interesting ruin of Old Buckhurst, is his-torically important for its association with the great and once-sump-tious Sackville family. They held Buckhurst since Henry II, a principle member being Thomas Sackville, Lord Buckhurst, first Earl of Dorset. Born at Withyham in 1536, he was Queen Elizabeth's Lord Treasurer, and part author of *Gorduboc*.

Withyham church was destroyed in 1663 by fire in a "tempest of thunder and lightning". If that tragedy had not happened, it would not be second to none in Sussex for the richness of its tombs. Many noble Sackville monuments perished in that family-named aisle, on the northern side, now no longer in existence. A large window in the Sackville chapel records the genealogy of a family now represented by Earl De la Warr. The main glory of this secluded church is the monument in the chapel to Thomas Sackville, youngest son of the fifth Earl, who died aged 13. The six brothers and six sisters of the youth, are depicted in bas-relief on the sides of the tomb, some as babies. The father, who was a poet, and one of the men who tried the judges of Charles I, died before the monument he had ordered for his

81

son was finished, so it represents a memorial to both. The sculptor was Gabriel Cibber.

At the turn of this century, Withyham had three bells made by John Waylett, an early 18th-century itinerant bell-founder. It is said he would call on the vicar and ask if anything was required. If a bell was cracked, or had to be replaced, he would dig a mould in a neighbouring field, build a fire, collect his metal, and do the work on the spot. Some called his trade 'higher tinkering'. At one time Sussex had 40 of his bells. Early in 1724, he stayed at Lewes, erected his furnace in the same way Benvenuto Cellini did in Florence in the 16th century, and started mending defective peels all over the place. He recast the old treble and made a new treble at Mayfield. Some church-wardens' records of those times prove that bell-founding was thirsty work! In *Historical Notes on Withyham*, some entries from parish accounts were reproduced by the then vicar, Mr. Sutton. Others, too amusing to omit, are:-

	£	s	d
For beer to the ringers when the Bell-founder was here		2	6
When the bell was weighed		3	6
When the bell was loaded		2	0
In carrying ye bell to Lewes and back again	1	10	0
When the bell was waid and hung up		3	0
For beer to the officers and several others a hanging up ye bell		18	0
In beer to the ringers when ye bell was hung		6	6

Rotherfield, to the south-east has Burne-Jones figures of outstanding beauty in a William Morris east window in its early 13th-century church. The village also has some fine houses, like the Old Manor, Oakdene, Rotherfield Hall, Bletchingly and Brook House, and, for final good measure, Argos Hill windmill, a post-mill with its sail.

The Saxons called Rotherfield *Ritheramfeld*, for it had more than one river to give it is name. The Rother rose in a cellar, and the Ouse was close by, though called *Sforda*, and linked with the sea at Seaford before the new Meeching haven emerged. The first church at Rotherfield was received as a thanksgiving from Berthoald, Duke of the South Saxons, who, a sick man, travelled to a French monastery dedicated to three saints, Dionysuis, Rusticus, and Eleutheris, whose bones were renowned for working miraculous cures. Berthoald recovered, and raised the early 13th-century St. Denys Church in honour of Dionysius. In his will, he threatened disaster to anyone who attempted to undermine the bequest. A translation of

Old Fireplace, Upper Parrock, Hartfield.

his will hangs in the church, signed and witnessed by several important Saxons, the last writing "I, Eanfric, have written, read over again, witnessed and signed ... "

Laughton is south-west of Heathfield, and Laughton Place was the original house of the Pelham family. According to tradition it was rebuilt in 1534 by Sir William Pelham, and given up for Halland, 1¼m. west of East Hoathly, where the Halland Park Farm has the remains of the Pelham mansion built in 1595 to replace Laughton Manor as the family's principal home, and a most unusual cast-iron-on-wood milestone stands on the London-Eastbourne road near Halland.

Like Wilmington Priory, beautiful Michelham Priory, founded in 1229 by Gilbert, grandson of Richer de l'Aigle, is the property of the Sussex Archaeological Trust. Today, it is one of the county's leading centres for craftmanship exhibitions. Built in the 13th and 14th centuries on an island site, the moat, seven acres in extent, encloses over six acres of land. It is fed by the Cuckmere, which flows through the fields to the north, east, and south of the priory. At the sluice-gates in the south-west corner, where there is a drop of 15 feet, the moat falls back into the Cuckmere, showing how the priory was built above flood level. It was a monastery of Augustinian Canons, their lives controlled by a Rule, or detailed series of regulations, originated by St. Augustine, Bishop of Hippo in North Africa around 390. They owed total allegiance to the Prior, elected by the whole community, and confirmed by the Bishop of Chichester. There is a legend that links Michelham with Thomas à Becket. Around 1150, the young Thomas was taken hunting by Richer de l'Aigle, who held the vast estate of the Rape of Pevensey, which included Michelham. The hunters came to a plank bridge across a mill stream. Richer crossed in safety, but Thomas's horse slipped, and he fell in the water. As he was swept towards the mill wheel only the timely shutting of the sluice gates saved him. The closing of the gates was afterwards believed to be the first miracle performed by Saint Thomas à Becket.

There are also some ghosts at Michelham, three people, a dog and a white horse. There is a total of 359 listed modern hauntings throughout the county and many of these are to be found in East Sussex. Among these are the Winchelsea Highwaymans' horses and the ghostly knight at Battle Abbey, seen by tourists in 1971. We also have moans and screams at Eridge Green in a barn where an unmarried pregnant girl hanged herself long ago.

No fewer than five ghosts have been seen at Michelham in recent years, the only tangible occult association being discovered in 1972.

Barbican House, Lewes.

A Bellarmine stone wine jar, often used in witchcraft practices, was found intact, containing what is thought to be a clay figure with several brass pins stuck in it. The image on the front of Bellarmine jars is a bearded character, purported to be a tongue-in-cheek cartoon of Bishop Bellarmini, who gained an evil reputation among medieval witches.

Herbert Pelham bought Michelham in 1587, then sold it later to Thomas Sackville, Earl of Dorset. An apparition at the priory is thought to be a Sackville. About five years ago, a lady wearing a grey dress and leading a small brown dog, was told at the ticket office that

85

dogs were not admitted. She turned back along the drive, then suddenly vanished within a few feet of the kiosk and the astounded attendant. She has since been seen between 11 a.m. and 5.30 p.m. A pair of ghosts was seen in 1969 in the main Tudor room on the ground floor. Two overseas visitors turned to relate the information on a wall notice to objects in the room. They saw a black-cloaked man's figure descend diagonally from the ceiling over the inglenook fireplace, and float gently through the end doorway. Even more startled, they saw a 'lady in a Tudor gown' glide past them from the adjoining room, then out through the same door. "It seemed as if she was chasing the man", one of the witnesses stated later.

Passing west through very delectable countryside one traverses Upper and Lower Dicker, an area once famed for Sussex pottery, and finds the great house called Firle Place en route.

There is a fine collection of pictures, porcelain and furniture at Firle Place, which has been open to the public since 1954. This followed redecoration and re-arrangement by the present Lord and Lady Gage, who returned after military occupation during the Second World War, and earlier occupation by a girls' school, to find that reinstatement was needed and that the management of such a large house had to be made easier. Until the latter part of the last century, the park came right up to the house. The balustrade and terrace were added by the present Lord Gage's father soon after he succeeded to the title.

The name East Firle occurred in the 13th century, but has now disappeared, and West Firle features on our maps. East Firle appears to have covered the part of the parish east of the park, and to have included Charleston and perhaps Heighton. The pre-Conquest manor of Firle, which belonged to the abbey of Wilton in Edward the Confessor's reign was "a very large one, of 48 hides and valued at £60". In 1086, it was part of the Sussex fee of the Count of Mortain, who had Pevensey Castle. From the reign of Edward II, or even earlier, West Firle was held by the Lyvets, and it remained theirs until 1440, when Thomas Lyvet "enfeoffed" Bartholomew Bolney in his manor. In the church are brasses to Bartholomew Bolney and his wife, Eleanor, who both died in 1476. Their daughter, Agnes, married William Gage, father of Sir John Gage of Firle, a member of a Gloucestershire family before they came to Sussex. But the Gages' connection with Sussex went back a generation earlier. The manor of West Firle was not acquired by the family until 1788, being purchased then from the Countess de Bruhl, heiress of the Chowns of Alfriston.

Anne of Cleves House, Lewes.

The Gage family have lived in this great house for some 500 years, first appearing in the 14th century when John Gage married Eleanor St. Clere, co-heiress of the Manor of Heighton St. Clere, Firle. The first notable member was Sir John Gage, whose company was much sought by Henry VIII, who left him £4,000, a princely sum in 1547, and made him a Council member during the minority of Edward VI. Another famous family name is that of General Thomas Gage, Commander-in-Chief of the British forces in America at the outbreak of the War of Independence which followed his skirmish in April 1775 at Lexington. Two months later he resigned after the Battle of Bunder's Hill. His brother, William Hall Gage, later Admiral of the Blue, was commended by Nelson for daringly capturing one ship and sinking a second in sight of the Spanish fleet.

Firle Place, though outwardly Georgian in appearance, has an early Tudor courtyard building. It is believed that early buildings and villages were sited at the foot of the Downs because of good water supplies from springs or wells. However, many large 16th-century houses were built there to profit from sheep-walks on the nearby hills. The soldier-courtier Sir John Gage, who died in 1556, had large flocks on Compton Down, at then-existing Exceat, and Friston, all these being listed in his will.

Firle is said to be the English home of the greengage, the first fruit having been brought home by botanist Thomas Gage, who planted it in the splendid gardens around the mansion, which still houses a chair and table used by Napoleon at St. Helena, and his gun. Nearby Firle Beacon rises to 718 feet above the sea. From its bases, East and West Sussex sweep away magnificently, with Kent some 30 miles away. Though not in Domesday, the lovely village of Glynde belonged to the Archbishop of Canterbury's Manor of Malling shortly after 1086, a house granted to the de Glynde family, who took their name from the peaceful village. Mount Caburn, one of the vast ramparts of the Downs, broods above Glynde. Its three acres have hollows in which relics have been found to such an extent it must have been a camping place for ancestors long before the advent of the Romans.

At one time, who would have dreamed of dressing up and going to an opera in the heart of the country? Today, Glyndebourne the world-famous opera house, and Glyndebourne the Tudor house, face one another across lawns which have weathered the "winds of change" for over 400 years. When John Christie's wild idea became a reality over 35 years ago, encouraged by his young operatic soprano wife, Audrey Mildmay, less than a dozen people got off the special train from Victoria to Lewes. Now, it is almost a matter of low cunning to get tickets, which have to be bought months ahead as, despite a longer summer season almost annually, the box office is always fully booked.

Firle Place.

The Theatre Royal, Brighton.

Interior room at Firle Place.

The opera house, designed by Edmund Warre, looks mellow now because John Christie, who was his own architect, spent years collecting weathered bricks and tiles in order to achieve the setting of his dreams. He inherited Glyndebourne and a fortune from his father, who built organs and did much estate work, on condition that he did something useful with his life. While working as a science master at Eton for 13 years, he developed his estate along medieval lines, with its own masons, wood-carvers and iron-workers. Edmund Warre also designed the additions to the Tudor House, which include a high, fine music room, complete with organ, a bay window, and tunnel vault with Elizabethan plasterwork. To the sound of beautiful music, add summer evenings, elegant black lace and flowing velvets or flower printed skirts and chiffon blouses, and you capture the dream of delight that is opera at Glyndebourne, where hampers of food and champagne cooling in the placid lake can be left quite safely during any performance.

The nearby small village of Ripe, with its Eckington Manor and yet another Pelham tower on St. John the Baptist Church, has a population of just over 300, and is rapidly becoming something of a hide-out for opera lovers.

7

UCKFIELD TO DITCHLING

Turning north-west from Hellingly, one finds Chiddingly and East Hoathly, within a maze of lanes. The latter boasts a church with one of the four stone ·spires in the county, and the remains of an Elizabethan mansion, Chiddingly Place, reputed to have an underground passage leading to the church. Alongside is a huge chapel barn, much older than the house, and with Tudor adaptations of fireplace and chimney. On to Framfield, with its goodly share of Sussex names, like Godman, Capel, Palmer, Tufton, Sackville and Courthope, where the church has a squint and the remains of a rood-loft, visible from the chancel steps, also a finely engraved brass to one Edward Gage. Dated 1595, it records his "*three sonnes and seaven daughters*".

Before reaching Uckfield, where Mount Ephraim was the original site of the present Cross-in-Hand largest post windmill in Sussex, digress to beautiful Sheffield Park whose gardens are owned by the National Trust. Beloved of artists, and situated midway between East Grinstead and Lewes, there are waterlilies on the five lakes at Sheffield Park, known earlier this century as the place where the Australians used to open their cricket season. Here runs the delightful Bluebell Railway between the park and Horsted Keynes, now in the western half of the county. The 18th-century house, once called Sheffield Place, was designed by James Wyatt, Controller of Public Works and Buildings in the reign of George III. The first Earl of Sheffield, John Baker Holroyd, was his patron as well as being a friend of Gibbon, the historian, who wrote *The Decline and Fall of the Roman Empire* in 1776 when only 39. The 80 acres of grounds were laid out at Sheffield Park in 1775 by Capability Brown, and modified in the 1930's.

Slightly north-east at Uckfield stands Buxted Park, with its famous trees and 13th-century church, where the weathercock over the shingled spire has been recording wind changes since 1665. The fine pine avenue was planted in 1777, and, among others, the church has a very rare brass of a 14th-century rector, one of the few existing with a figure in the middle of a cross.

Buxted is not recorded before 1298, but does have the reputation of having cast the first cannon ever made in England, though some say it was at Maresfield, which lies south-west at Nutley, with its 18th-century Shelley Arms and windmill. Wordsworth's brother was a rector of Buxted for 50 years, and is buried in the churchyard. It is recorded that in the early 1800's, it had a labourer called George Watson. Although almost an imbecile, he had such an amazingly tenacious memory he was unable to forget anything he had once seen, or any fact or figure repeated to him.

On 30th July, 1966, Buxted Park was opened as a lavish health hydro in the presence of a distinguished gathering. The owners, Kenneth and Heather Shipman, spent over £600,000 on the stately home in its 325-acre estate, and the hydro was opened in a most unusual way. A section of the Royal Philharmonic Orchestra gave a gala concert within the portico of the great Georgian house, originally built by Thomas Medley, whose finely carved rococo arms are over the chimney-piece in the Grand Hall. Part of the interior was destroyed by fire in 1940. The owner then was the Hon. Nellie Ionides, whose husband, Basil Ionides, famed as an architect and interior decorator, rebuilt the interior, made a new entrance on the west side, and removed the top storey.

Buxted Park has many royal associations. In 1845, Queen Victoria, her mother, the Duchess of Kent, and Prince Albert, stayed as guests of Lord Liverpool, the then owner. During the time of Mr. and the Hon. Mrs. Ionides, Queen Mary was a constant visitor, perhaps because the Queen and her hostess shared an interest in collecting porcelain.

Fletching, with its *Rose and Crown Inn* where so many art exhibitions are held, its ancient buildings, including St. Mary and St. Andrew Church, with its Norman west tower with twin bell-openings and later shingled broach spire, is not far from Buxted Park. Piltdown is 1 mile south-east. Haywards Heath, Lindfield and Cuckfield are all in some proximity to Sheffield Park, and though all now come under the aegis of West Sussex County Council, they deserve inclusion for county reasons. The first took advantage of the London to Brighton railway line when it opened in 1841, but Cuckfield, an important town in former times, and Lindfield, a wealthy residential district, both declined its amenities. Some allege the name Haywards Heath is linked with the highwayman, or some man named Hay-ward, but this is not substantiated. The name was first mentioned in 1261 as Heyworth. 'Worth' meant a small enclosure and 'hey' was either hay, or an old English word meaning 'hedge'. The first mention of the second half of the name was in 1554, when it appeared as 'hoth', the Sussex form of Heath. The first time 'heath' was mentioned was in 1603, when there is a reference to Hewards Hethe. As these references apply to any other similar word in the county, they are perhaps permissible.

It is interesting to learn that barges could once negotiate the Ouse higher upstream than Lindfield, at that time in East Sussex, as were Haywards Heath and Cuckfield, where moorhens can be seen jerking their heads in shy fashion, and kingfishers dart around. Some locks and weirs were built in 1769, others in 1811. Cargoes were thus carried by waterways almost to Cuckfield before the railway era. Because it was not profitable, this delightful 'navigation' fell into disuse in 1868.

Close to Lindfield, which certainly has one of the finest village streets in the county, stands a stately mansion called Buxshalls, now an old peoples' home. The death took place at Buxshalls on 16th February, 1917, of a redoubtable British soldier, Lieutenant Colonel Dudley Sampson, J.P. Depty Lieutenant for Sussex, who married Katherine Mary Jollands, of Buxshalls, in 1878. On his grandmother's side, Colonel Sampson was descended from the de Garenciers, an old Norman family, and on his mother's side from the de Warennes, who owned vast tracts of Sussex under William the Conqueror, including Lewes Castle. There are memorial tablets to this outstanding soldier-poet in the chapel at Buxshalls, and one in memory of Colonel Sampson's eldest son, Dudley de Garenciers Jollands Sampson, who died of typhoid, aged 17, at Potsdam, Germany, on 14th November, 1899.

The village of Ditchling lies in the shadow of Ditchling Beacon, one of the highest peaks in the South Downs. The Romans had a camp at the top, and Ditchling may still be reached by going down the 800-foot half-subterranean path our conquerors dug, so devised that a regiment might descend into the Weald. On the top of the Beacon can be found one of the dewponds which are dotted all over Sussex. Contrary to many opinions, research seems to prove that these circular, shallow pools of water are not mysterious. Hardly a man who made them, or a shepherd who tended his sheep in former times, probably carrying an iron crook made at Pyecombe Forge, ever knew them by any other name than 'sheep-ponds', or more vernacularly, 'ship-ponds'.

Even in the hottest summer, and on the highest Downland, these ponds, like the widow's cruse, are never empty. Once, in company with a Mr. Pickard, former steward of the Glyne estate, the writer Arthur Beckett visited an old man called Weller who lived in a Glynde cottage. A dewpond builder, he was raised in his father's and grandfather's traditions, and he said the pond lining was "two courses of mortar and two of flints, in alternate layers". During rains, water flowed in by means of the natural channels in the hills, passing through a simply-constructed filter on the outer rim of the pond. Generally six feet deep in the centre, and sixty feet in diameter, they had an additional border of concrete, twenty to thirty feet wide. When there were large sheep stocks on the Downs, 500 sheep could be watered daily at such a pond without, under normal conditions, seriously diminishing the water supply.

Alfred the Great once had a park at Ditchling, and Anne of Cleves lived in the cross-shaped village in the still beautiful half-timbered Anne of Cleves House with its Tudor chimneys. One gets a fine view of Clayton's Jack and Jill windmills across the common, where the Ditchling gibbet used to stand, railed round with a cockerel on the top. It was a grim reminder of the day in 1734 when they hanged Jacob Harris, a Jewish pedlar of astounding turpitude, after he had murdered three people at a Ditchling Common Inn, then plundered their house. He was hanged at Horsham, as a lesson for all, suspended on the gibbet, of which the stake called Jacob's Post on the common was a reminder. His bones hung there till they fell to pieces, a grim warning indeed! Now, thankfully, the gibbet has gone the same way.

It is recorded that as all gibbets are "good" for something, "a piece of Jacob's Post carried on a person is sovran against toothache". One Sussex archaeologist tells of an old woman who lived for over eighty years on Ditchling Common whose belief was so great that she carried a splinter of Jacob's Post in a pocket long after her teeth had gone!

There has always been a fierce desire to keep the villages of Ditchling and Keymer apart. Within living memory, a Keymer youth courting a Ditchling girl risked a ducking in a water-butt outside the *Bull Inn*. This difficulty has now been resolved by the new division of the county which has firmly placed Keymer in West Sussex. At the turn of the century it was still a common sight to see oxen yoked to the plough. The reason was their ability to work on wet soil into which horses would sink.

In 1312 Edward II granted a weekly market to be held in the village on Tuesdays, and a charter for a Fair on the Eve, Feast and Morrow of St. Margaret of Antioch, to whom the lovely church is dedicated, with its pre-Norman nave and central tower and chancel added in the 13th century by the Cluniac monks at Lewes Priory.

In 1822 the Horticultural Society was founded, and held the first Gooseberry and Currant Show, Stoolball Match and Kettle Feast. Prizes were offered that year for the best faggot stack, the best pig in a stye, the cleanest cottage, plus those for fruit and vegetables. The show is still held annually.

For years, Sir Frank Brangwyn lived and painted at Ditchling. Sculptor Eric Gill, also responsible for the famous Gill Typeface, arrived in 1907, and founded the Guild of St. Joseph and St. Dominic on the Common. The Ditchling Press, renowned for its exquisite hand-printing, was founded by Hilary Pepler. Hilary Pepler, who owned Hopkin's Crank when Eric Gill left, believed that the land for the house and garden had been enclosed from the Common as a burial ground for some of the dead from the Battle of Lewes.

The great Shakespearean actress, Ellen Terry, stayed in Ditchling several times, and one evening held an audience spellbound with her famous "Quality of Mercy" speech.

In 1794 a regular coach service from London to Brighton went through Ditchling, with a pause for a change of horses at the *Bull Inn* prior to the stiff climb up the Borstal, an old word meaning a hill. Toll-gates were put at the north and south ends of the village. An old lady lived at the north end who was a great opium smoker. As there were no restrictions on its sale in those 18th-century days, she used to get her supplies quite easily at the local shop!

There is a striking line of trees in a 'V'-shape, planted to commemorate the Victorian era jubilee. The 13th-century church stands near a great yew, and in it are three stone coffin lids some 600 years old. In the chancel is the old pitch pipe with which the choir was given the note before the organ music started. On a modern note, we have artist Margaret Milne's internationally famous Ditchling Gallery in the quaint, winding street. There is also the artists' Attic Club, originally started in an attic, and the rich cluster of craftsmen and craftswomen in the Ditchling Guild, and other groups.

A famous Ditchling resident is Vera Lynn, who became a Dame of the British Empire on 14th June, 1975, and has lived there for over 20 years. Two other East Sussex figures renowned in the world of entertainment received honours on the same occasion. Comedian Sandy Powell, known as Mr. Eastbourne after he appeared on stage at Eastbourne Pier every summer between 1948 and 1965, was awarded the

M.B.E. The O.B.E. was given to actress Fay Compton, of Hove, which boasts another D.B.E., Dame Jean Rivette-Drake, former Director of the W.R.A.C.

In May, 1976, the world-renowned actress, Dame Flora Robson, moved from her Kemp Town home to Wykeham Terrace, near the Victorian Clock Tower, Western Road and the busy Churchill Square complex. Now retired, she is deeply involved with many activities in the town, including Brighton Theatre Group, founded in 1968 by the well-known producer Miss Mavis Ward, whose father, Mr. Harry Ward, founded Brighton and Hove operatic Society in 1886. Wykeham Terrace, built in the early 19th century, is reputed to have its own ghost, a headless woman dressed in grey, who wanders from the nearby St. Nicholas' Church graveyard, and disappears into one of the houses with a tower in the section of the terrace recently renovated.

On an amusing note, it seems almost incredible that this peaceful, unassuming village was the scene of constant smuggling. At one time, the entire choir was engaged in the nefarious trade. It is good to report that, unlike the Suffolk village of Richangles, they did not go so far as to hustle the kegs for hiding into the safe-keeping of the pulpit during the sermon. It is recorded, however, that while all this was going on, "the congregation kept its eyes cast piously Heavenwards". In 1774, a party of 400 men and 200 laden packhorses passed through Ditchling on their way from Cuckmere Haven. Mothers, it is said, told their children to "watch the wall while the Gentlemen go by". It is not recorded whether they obeyed obediently.

Finally, Ditchling is the East Sussex village which achieved considerable publicity on the purchase of land for a village green by The Friends of Ditchling for over £10,000. It is almost certainly the only village in England ever to have taken such a positive and costly step in the promotion of its beauty and appearance.

LEWES TO BRIGHTON

Lewes, Newhaven, with Seaford, and Brighton make a kind of geographical triangle, and the Downs usurp the scene between the two river valleys east of Lewes. There is a kind of ageless wisdom about the treeless heights ranging from Ditchling Beacon east past the profiles of Firle Beacon and Mount Caburn, then beyond the terraced slopes of Lewes to haunts eastwards to Beachy Head.

Within the triangle lie ages of history in such villages as Beddingham, Barcombe and Southease, whose bridge spans the Ouse halfway between Lewes and Newhaven, just where the ebb tide flows fast, sometimes at eight knots. Southease church has a noted Norman round flint tower. There are only three in Sussex, and all are in East Sussex, the others being at Lewes and Piddinghoe, pronounced *Pidd'nhoo*, with its sailing and Deans Farm Estate. The house was built in the early 17th century for Lord Chief Justice Heath, is listed as a building of architectural and historic interest, and is mainly constructed of flint with brick quoins under a tiled roof. One of Piddinghoe's quaintest possessions is a head on one of the church's nave walls. There for centuries, it has preached a bad gospel, "seeing nothing and saying too much, having shut its eyes and opened its mouth".

Telscombe village is a shy, unchanged place resting smugly in its combe above Piddinghoe, which has tended to suffer from proximity to commercialised Newhaven. Fortunately, Telscombe, set deep in its seclusion, has little to do with the bungaloid aridity that is Telscombe Cliffs. Its flint St. Laurence Church has a Norman nave and chancel and an unbuttressed west tower. The village, sited in a snug dip in the Downs, shelters among screening beeches, and clusters around its church, which also has a 13th-century font and a window well over 500 years old. The register records the 1819 burial of the last man hanged in England for sheep stealing. Telscombe's main benefactor was Ambrose Gorham, who made a fortune as a book-

97

The Black Horse, Rottingdean.

maker, and greatly improved the life of the village. The 1902 Grand National was won by his horse, Shannon Lass.

The first village out of Lewes on the Newhaven road is Kingston, one of three of the same name in Sussex, set on the side of a hill that once belonged to Sir Philip Sidney. Next comes Iford, with straw still blowing about the cows in its quiet meadows, and lovely Rodmell, whose manor house was given to Anne Boleyn by Henry VIII, and where Virginia Woolf spent happy days amid bouts of despair at Monks House. The prettiest house in the small flint village is the early Victorian rectory. In the 13th-century church of St. Peter is a big square font made of Sussex marble, believed to be nearly one thousand years old. There is a mysterious dewpond at the nearby hamlet of Northease which may go back to the Stone Age. It is said that its peculiar preparation secures a lower temperature which leads to filling by condensation, either of dew or moisture from low-lying clouds. Two lovers lie under a tombstone in the churchyard. The young man died trying to save a dog from drowning 150 years ago,

98

and the young woman with him died of grief. Another grave has a mill-stone over it, and the last miller of Rodmell lies beneath.

Ringmer to the north-east of Lewes has happy associations with the great naturalist Gilbert White, and his noteworthly tortoise, Timothy. Gilbert often stayed at Ringmer with his enchantingly-named aunt Rebecca Snooke, who lived at Delves House and married a son of the Vicar of Ringmer. Under the name of Northdelve, the house is mentioned in 1340 in the Ringmer Court Rolls, and there, too, lived Gilbert White's tortoise, whose portrait is painted on a signpost leading to the church. Often "in pursuit of natural knowledge" on the coast of Newhaven, the famous writer's association with Ringmer is marked on the village sign, which also shows links with John Harvard, married at Lewes, and William Penn, the great Quaker, who married Ringmer-born Gulielma Posthuma Springett. She was born after the death at twenty-three of her father, Sir William Springett, a colonel during the siege of Arundel Castle, whose bust is in Ringmer Church. The story of her mother's nightmare journey by coach to reach her dying husband at Arundel just before Gulielma's birth makes stirring reading.

Those who would like to modernise Lewes, pronounced *Lewis*, would do well to remember that its charm would inevitably vanish the moment such changes were allowed. Nothing supports this belief

Carved staircase in Lewes Town Hall.

more than the fact that the ancient and historical county town of Sussex, now the seat of government of the newly-constructed East Sussex County Council, was venerable and grey before Brighton, then Brighthelmstone, was even thought of. After all, it was a Lewes man who discovered Brighton, Dr. Russell, (1759), whose grave is in South Malling churchyard. Many historical curiosities, collected by members of Sussex Archaeological Society, are preserved in Lewes Castle. In a beautiful and sun-blessed situation, its medley of twisting streets and old buildings climbs the steep slopes to its hilltop Norman castle. It is also interesting to record that, like Greenwich, and Tema in Ghana, Lewes stands fair and square on the meridian.

As an old prescriptive Borough which was incorporated in 1881, Lewes has been prominent in Sussex history since Saxon time; 14th May, 1265, was an important date for the town, when Henry III's forces were beaten by the barons, led by Simon de Montfort, in the Battle of Lewes. The Priory, the King's headquarters, and the Castle capitulated, and the famous treaty, the *Mise of Lewes*, was sealed at the Priory, and is often cited as the beginning of parliamentary government.

Old view in Lewes of Southover High Street, looking east past St. John's Church with Anne of Cleves House in foreground.

The Grange, Rottingdean.

After impoverishment when the de Warenne family faded in the 14th century, Lewes began to prosper again, and its grammar school was founded. The Town Book also dates from then. When Civil war arose in the 17th century Lewes witnessed much ecclesiastical unrest. Today, there are seven churches, of which I shall mention just two. St. John the Baptist at Southover contains the leaden caskets of William de Warenne and his Norman wife, Gundrada, one of the Conqueror's daughters. The discovery of their coffins by workmen excavating for Lewes railway station alongside the walls of the 11th-century Priory of St. Pancras, first of the Cluniac Order to be founded in England, compensates for what many still regard as modern vandalism, however much justification is attempted. The other church is St. Michael's at South Malling, rebuilt in 1628 adjacent to the site of a Saxon monastery founded in the 8th century, some remains of an earlier building being incorporated in the tower. The register records the marriage of John Harvard in 1636, founder of

Harvard University, and there is a memorial to Dr. Russell of Brighton sea water fame.

A multitude of historic places at Lewes include Anne of Cleves House at Southover, a fine medieval house now used as a folk museum, the Barbican House, headquarters of Sussex Archaeological Society, and Museum, near the Castle entrance and Bull House in High Street. With all these in mind, and much left unrecorded, it is amusing to reflect that the old address of a visitor to Brighton used to read "at Brighthelmstone, near Lewes". The point is equally proved in the pages of "*The Sussex Weekly Advertiser; or Lewes Journal*" of some 150 years, or more, ago, when it published long columns of Lewes news, but only brief paragraphs of Brighton correspondence.

Lewes Town Hall has a truly magnificent carved staircase, culled from Slaugham Manor now in West Sussex, its little panels representing the elements and the senses. Among countless curious things in the ancient town we can certainly include the grave of William Huntington in the burial ground of the Jireh chapel at Cliffe. He was an eccentric evangelist and founder of a sect called the Huntingtonians. His life story has a Dick Whittington element about it. Born at Lewes in 1745, he acquired a smattering of learning at the local grammar school, after which he became successively errand boy, ostler, cobbler, coal-heaver, tramp and itinerant preacher. Eventually, he settled at Mortlake, assumed the name of Hungtington, avowed a conviction of sin and conversion, then added the initials S.S. to his name, indicating that he was a 'sinner saved'. Uncultured, rude and vulgar, he wielded great power over his congregations and their purses! For the last 25 years of his life, his Providence Chapel in Gray's Inn Lane, London, was regularly packed each Sunday. In 1808, he married Lady Sanderson, widow of a Lord Mayor of London. It is said she fell in love with him years earlier when he was a coal-heaver passing her home on his way to work. At her request, Huntington built her a home between Cranbrook and Staplehurst in Kent, and called it *My Lady's Cottage*. He died in 1813 while visiting Tunbridge Wells, and was brought back to Cliffe in Lewes for burial. His incredible epitaph, composed by himself, reads:

> Here lies the coal-heaver who departed this life in the 69th year of his age, beloved of his God but abhorred of men. The Omniscient Judge at the Grand Assize shall ratify and confirm this to the confusion of many thousands, for England and its metropolis shall know that there hath been a prophet among them.

North End House, Rottingdean.

Lewes Town Bell is called Gabriel, and is inscribed with the Archangel's name. Dated mid-16th century, it was rung to mark the granting of a Successor Parish Council status to the County Town. Formerly a church bell, Gabriel has hung in the Market Town in Market Street since 1972, and is rung on notable national and local occasions.

For gourmet satisfaction and social pleasure, Lewes has two rendezvous of distinction, *Shelleys Hotel* and *The Pelham Arms*, the latter being one of the most attractive pubs in the area and said to own a poltergeist. Also known as *Sussex Kitchen*, it is a white building with black accents and a traditional façade.

The current craze for colour prints in the home has resulted from the work of the famous Lewes-born printer and engraver, George Baxter, whose works are prized throughout the world. He was born in 1804 just after his father had founded a printing and publishing business in the town's hilly, gabled High Street. He served his apprenticeship in a North Street, Brighton, bookseller's, during which time he began experimenting with colour reproductions from wood blocks. In 1835, in London, he was granted a patent for his work, and produced a celebrated book of paintings called "*Cabinet of Paintings*". He really attained fame after producing a colour print of butterflies, but did not achieve much financial success. There is a collection of Baxter's colourful but homely prints in Lewes Public Library.

Lewes is the third, moving westwards, of the vast Rapes of East Sussex, the others being Hastings and Pevensey. There are three in the western area, namely Chichester, Arundel and Bramber, and the history of the six is fascinating. One has to dip back to the decay of Roman times and the incoming might of the Normans to find the Rapes' roots. The Conqueror chose the sea-girt parts for the establishment of his empire, disdaining a march through the Weald, which was never a *military* obstacle, not, for all the talk, the "impenetrable forest" it was made out to be. What it did was retain within Sussex all its ideas, speech and folk-lore, and maintain its isolation down the centuries to fairly modern times. William, astute and powerful, recognised this, so set about securing his communications and, via Dover, took the north-east road through Kent, garrisoning every harbour on his way to London, thus following a line of invasion, commerce, and foreign travel, that has existed from the very origins of our history.

It is firmly recorded that nowhere had the remains of Roman civilisation decayed more than in Sussex. The resultant admixture of old British and Teutonic bloods had formed a population which is observable today in Sussex villages, where so many people are short, with dark, piercing eyes, and a few are tall and large, with the slow walk, heavy bodies and light hair of the marsh men from Frisia and the Baltic.

Soon after the sharp Norman brains and Norman power arrived, the re-organisation of Sussex began. As always, it stemmed from the sea. The county was carved up into administrative divisions called Rapes, a name that stems from 1086, and whose etymology is dubious. The Normans, being logical, created definite boundaries where there had been nothing but indefinable limits to the county's separate parts. However, the general set of divisons was certainly inherited by the Normans from an older, semi-barbaric state. It took a long time for *actual* divisions to be clarified, a classic case taking place in the western area, where, for centuries, Slindon was bandied about between the Arundel and Chichester Rapes, finally coming to rest with the latter.

For each Rape, a town which could be reached by ships was selected as the basis for the division. As always, the Channel tides seemed to be the creators of the county. The importance assigned to Sussex is shown in the fact that William chose men all connected

104

with his family to receive the Rapes, not as proprietors but military overlords over a vast number of manors. Their names were Montgomery, Braose, Warren and Moreton. It has been said that if an exact calculation could be taken, with the exception of the counties Palatine, nowhere was feudal power more concentrated than on this stretch of the coast of England.

Probably the foundation of its monasteries was the main factor in the early economic life of East Sussex, but the establishment of its three Rapes comes second, and the Lewes Rape, delivered into the de Warenne hands, takes precedence. Its development took some 200 years, and spread from the ancient capital, presumably fed from the equally ancient harbour, then gradually extended north over the Weald, and later straddled across the northern boundary of the Forest Ridge. Such development was natural when we consider its boundaries, with the Ouse to the east and Adur to the west, and the strip of land running north between the two river valleys. Lewes was its Rape's vital core, and is, today, still fairly unchanged.

On March 1, 1977, it was announced that the Queen had approved the appointment of a monk, Father Peter John Ball, Prior of the Community of the Glorious Ascension, whose mother house is at Cleeve Priory, Watchet, Somerset, to be Suffragan Bishop of Lewes in the diocese of Chichester. Father Peter is only the second monk to become a Bishop since the Reformation, and it is the first time since the 1920's that the Crown has chosen a member of a religious community to be a Church of England Bishop in this country.

In this context, a fleeting return to Pevensey and Hastings is permissible. The former's name is probably derived from Celtic roots, signifying "the fortification at the far end of the wood". Here, as in the case of Hastings, yet unlike any other Rape, that of Pevensey was actually upon the sea. It is also a curious shape, narrowing a bit towards the middle, then bulging out towards the top, or north end. Normally, these Sussex divisions have their important part on the sea coast. The Pevensey Rape's outline is supposed to stem from the iron industry having developed to the north long before the Conquest.

The Rape of Hastings has its own pecularities, arising from it being at the narrow eastern end of Sussex where no hinterland of Weald country assists the normal development of a Rape.

Let us leave Lewes for Newhaven and Seaford on a richly rural note — that of Sussex sheep bells, of which many fine examples can be seen in Anne of Cleves House. Shepherds had various methods of counting the number of sheep that went through the hurdles. One method used the following words:-

one-erum, two-erum, cock-erum, shu-erum, sith-erum,
sath-erum, wineberry, wagtail, tarry diddle, den.

Den meant that 20 sheep had passed throught the hurdles. Bells were placed on *leaders*, those who were known to stray, and where mists might prevail. The bells often had unusual names, and made various sounds. There were Lewes bells, made many years ago of sheet iron, and one of the few bells made with brazed sides instead of the customary riveting. Robert Wells was a famous bell-maker in the 18th and 19th centuries, but the foundry has gone, taken over in 1825 by Mears and Stainforth (The Whitechapel Bell Foundry, Ltd., of 32 Whitechapel Road, London, E.1., founded in 1570). They no longer make sheep bells, but have a set of "Lewes" bells on show.

'Can' or 'canister' bells were widely used in East Sussex, and were made of sheet iron. The 'note' of each was a 'chance' affair. Those called 'cluckets' or 'clunck' bells were 'ridged' on the top, and had crown staples. It is recorded that these bells took their name from their 'cluck-cluck' sound. 'Tongues' were made in varied shapes and are called 'clappers', 'clippers' or 'knockers'. In "*Much Ado About Nothing*", Shakespeare wrote: "He hath a heart as sound as a bell, and his tongue is the clapper, or what his heart thinks his tongue speaks". It is sad to reflect that one day such sounds may well have vanished from East Sussex for ever.

*   *   *

From Lewes to Newhaven is about eight miles. Some may consider the journey uninteresting, but I would disagree. It is true that the landscape traverses the flat and lonely levels between Beddington and Iford Hill, but there are always the Downs for distant joy, and, like David Harrison in his '*Along the South Downs*', I can find a "certain beauty" in the white spectre of the former cement works. Iford Hill affords fine views, with a Bronze Age settlement about a mile from sleepy Tarring Neville. Little remains today except holes for hut-posts unearthed during excavation. After its medieval name of Midewinde, or the 'middle winding river', the Ouse became known as 'The Water of Lewes', but, like other rivers, it changed its direction near its mouth, and no longer joins with the sea at Seaford.

It does, in fact, reach the sea in one of the finest stretches of unspoiled coastline in the country, and here we find the busy, colourful port of Newhaven, with its wonderfully "fishy" harbour dominated by a high chalk cliff and protected by a breakwater, extending 2,400 feet out to sea, on the western side. This, with the lighthouse at

Chain Pier, Brighton, destroyed in a storm in 1896.

the end, is a delightful feature, and easily accessible to motorists as there is adequate parking space on the west promenade. On the eastern side is the East Pier, extending 1,400 feet seawards.

The fishing industry at Newhaven is important and expanding. There is first-class angling, and, in summer, yachtsment populate the harbour, where in 1962 Cresta Marine Limited opened its first yacht marina on the south coast. Now one of the largest in the country, it can accommodate up to 250 boats in deep water moorings, and 350 boats in the boat park, with full supporting facilities.

Newhaven Lifeboat Station is one of the oldest in the country, established in 1803, the same year in which Rye started, it has a record of well over 450 lives saved. Newhaven Lifeboatmen have won 18 medals for gallantry, and the present Lifeboat 'Kathleen Mary' was named by the Duchess of Kent on 13th July, 1959. Eastbourne Station started in 1822, and Hastings in 1858.

Formerly known as Meeching, the town owes its present name to the change of the course of the Ouse in the 16th century, the river having previously entered the sea near the *Buckle Inn* just west of Seaford. The church of St. Michael is in Church Hill, leading to Meeching Down, from which there is a fine view north-west towards

Lewes. Nearly 900 years old, it is believed to be one of the first Norman churches ever built in England. Very rare in the entire country is the way the chancel is formed in the lower stages of the tower. It is believed to be a copy of an ancient church still existing at Yainville, on the banks of the Seine in Normandy.

There is an epitaph in St. Michael's churchyard which deserves a brief account. It is on the grave of a Newhaven brewer called Thomas Tipper, (1785) who brewed ale known as 'Newhaven Tipper'. The words were written by Thomas 'Clio' Rickman, friend and biographer of notorious Tom Paine, assocated with Lewes and author of *The Rights of Man*. Lewes, I discovered, was not always proud of Tom Paine, and Cuckfield went further. A report in the *Sussex Advertiser* of 1793 says Cuckfield "emphasised its loyalty to the constitution by singing 'God save the King' in the streets and burning Paine in effigy". Thomas 'Clio' Rickman, who died in 1834, was the great-great uncle of Frederick L. Griggs, who wrote "*Highways and Byways in Sussex*". He wore a hat like a beehive, wrote some execrable verse, but produced the Newhaven epitaph which was greatly admired by Charles Lamb.

> Reader, with kind regard this grave survey,
> Nor heedless pass where TIPPER'S ashes lay,
> Honest, he was, ingenious, blunt and kind,
> And dared do, what few dare do, speak his mind,
> Philosophy and history well he knew,
> Was versed in physickl and in surgery too;
> The best old Stingo he both brewed and sold,
> Nor did one knavish act to get his gold,
> He played through life a varied part,
> And knew immortal Hudibras by heart,
> Reader, in real truth, such was the Man,
> Be better, wiser, laugh more if you can.

It is believed that Newhaven Tipper emerged in order to contest the supremecy of an Eastbourne brew called Rug, something for which one would search vainly today in the town. The 17th-century water poet, John Taylor, described as being "the prey of lease and the law", visited Sussex between August 9 and September 3, 1653. At Eastbourne, he found the brew called Eastbourne Rug, and wrote this doggerel to it:-

> No cold can ever pierce his flesh or skin
> Of him who is well lin'd with Rug within;
> Rug is a Lord beyond the Rules of Law,

It conquers hunger in a greedy maw,
And, in a word, of all drinks potable,
Rug is most puissant, potent, botable.
Rug was the Capital Commander there,
And his Lieutenant-General was strong beer.

As an educational centre, Seaford has long been known for its many boys' preparatory schools. Now an Urban District Council, it has a shingle beach that is excellent for bathing. Steady growth has taken place since the last war, and the town has splendid library facilities. To the east, Seaford Head rises above the town. Bought for preservation by the U.D. Council, they have laid out a fine 18-hole golf course with striking views. Seaford has a long history, Roman and pre-Roman remains having been found, particularly on Seaford Head. In 1854, a gold medal inscribed to Antonia, sister of Mark Anthony, was picked up on the beach at low tide.

On 7th November 1974, over a century of Newhaven's history ended with the official opening of a landmark for East Sussex County Council — a new £1 million swing bridge. It resulted from severe traffic congestion on the A259 through Newhaven, with its

Famous yew tree in Wilmington churchyard.

narrow twisting high street, the old swing bridge and level crossing over the railway.

The old bridge, dating from 1864, had long been inadequate, subject to a weight restriction of 8 tons and a speed limit of 10 m.p.h. Heavy vehicles wishing to cross the River Ouse were obliged to make a detour of up to 15 miles.

The southern section of the ring road was opened to traffic in August, 1972, and work started on the new swing bridge in November, 1972. The swing bridge is of steel box girder construction 154 feet (47m) long and carrying a 24 feet (7.32m) wide carriageway and two cantilevered footways, each 8 feet (2.44m) wide. It turns to give a navigation channel of 60 feet (18.3m) wide between fenders. The pivot bearing, on which the bridge turns, is on the east side of the Ouse, giving a span of 98 feet (30m) over the navigation channel and 56 feet (17m) over the east bank.

*   *   *

Out of the mists of East Sussex time, Woodingdean, Ovingdean and Rottingdean have names that exhale Saxon echoes. Once self-contained and cosily happy in their rural seclusion, they are now beset by builders and motor traffic. In particular, Saltdean is a house agent's paradise, with its sea-blue Lido and excellent community centre overlooked by the green-and-white, round-windowed house where the late Sir George Robey, "Prime Minister of Mirth" and Lady Robey (awarded the O.B.E. on 14th June 1975) once lived.

The late H.S. Toms, a fine archaeologist who was curator of Brighton Museum from 1906 to 1939, stated there were many burials by cremation in the valley that belonged to Early Iron Age and Romano-British times. One ancient British cremation was actually found in the cliff edge of Saltdean valley. In 1912, interesting coins were washed out of the cliffs, and identified as a 'first brass' of Antonius Pius, struck after his death in 161, a silver denarius of Trajan similar to one struck during the time of Julius Caesar, and really the forerunner of the old one penny.

When an ancient burial ground was discovered at Saltdean in 1923, the interest of the archaeological world descended on the district. Excavations for road material revealed a mound of 150 tons of flints. Upon their removal, a floor came to light of extremely hard mould. Pieces of pottery lay in one corner, also cremated bones and worked flints. These were assessed as belonging to the latter portion of the Bronze Age.

110

The beach and cliffs at Rottingdean.

In 1587, Saltdean was suggested as a defence provision against the Spanish Armada. In one of the first historical references to a place of which it has been said, "Young people will not live there and old people cannot die there", the then Deputy Lieutenant for Sussex suggested that "a trenche with sunken flankers for small shotte" should be built there. The Spaniards and the Dutch were driven off several times at Saltdean Gap, and when in 1794 the Government thought of erecting a barracks in the area, Saltdean bottom was one of the sites considered. It was there that the Duke of Cumberland reviewed all the troops stationed on the Sussex coast during the wars against the French. Made by Brighton Corporation, there is a magnificent undercliff walk from Saltdean to Brighton, something which is being preserved in the construction of Brighton Marina. The air is reputed to be very healthy. There is a belt of seaweed off Telscombe Tye which charges the air with iodine! Saltdean Vale was smugglers' road from the beach. Today, it leads to a colony of residences called the Mount, situated in the area's most sheltered part.

Telscombe Cliffs and Peacehaven are not so easy on the eye, though improved by better side roads and avenues. Skip past them and make for Ovingdean, where St. Wulfran's small flint church

111

takes us back, thankfully, to Saxon and Norman times and a present query. What is the answer to the puzzling fact of a pointed blank arch in the chancel north wall, visible inside a 1907 chapel which replaces a medieval one? The arch is cut into by the Toman window, and includes a lower low-side lancet. One supposition is that there had been a decision to open the wall for the chapel, then it had been relinquished. The suggestion has been put forward by Canon B.J. Scott, that it may have been connected with hurried repairs after the 1377 French raids. Who can tell?

A little way back to the south-east lies lovely, ancient Rotting-dean, where Sir William Watson, the last of the great Victorian poets, lived in a cottage on the State pension of £200 a year with his wife and two daughters. Known as an "Old Contemptible of Song", he was born in 1858 and died in a Ditchling nursing home in 1935. Many famous people have lived in the village, among them Rudyard Kipling, who left The Elms because he was pestered by sight-seeing crowds, and Stanley Baldwin, whose wife, Lucy, lived in the house which later became the Dene Hotel, with her father, Edward Rids-dale. The hotel was sold in 1975 for use as a retirement home for teachers, and is now owned by the Retired Teachers' Housing Asso-ciation of London.

The pond and green, with St. Margaret's Church facing west across the latter's soft turf, still remain the centre of village life. On the west side stands North End House, once the home of Kipling's "Beloved Aunt Georgia", wife of Sir Edward Burne-Jones, seven of whose magnificent stained-glass windows can be seen in the church. In 1923, Sir Roderick Jones, head of Reuter's, bought North End House. It was formed by joining Prospect House and Aubrey Cot-tage. Sir Edward died there in 1898, his ashes, together with those of his wife, now reposing in a wall niche at St. Margaret's. Today, Sir Roderick Jones' widow, authoress and playwright Enid Bagnold,

Centre of Rottingdean in Victorian times, with *Old White Horse* Hotel in centre.

still lives there, immersed in Rottingdean's many activities. She received the C.B.E. in the 1976 New Year's Honours List in recognition of her numerous classics. These included "National Velvet" (which made actress Elizabeth Taylor a star) and the evergreen "The Chalk Garden", so cherished by professional and amateur theatrical companies.

Mentioned in Domesday, the great historical background to Rottingdean now rests firmly on protection against the sophistication that is Brighton. This is largely due to the dedicated work of the local Preservation Society, which, with Heinemanns, the publishing house now using the famous landmark as its trademark, restored the black-tarred, hooded windmill on Beacon Hill, so named because it was used as a warning point against the Armada.

Two pupils at St. Aubyn's School became famous. One was the Duke of Wellington, the other was Cardinal Manning, Archdeacon of Chichester in 1840, who entered the Roman Catholic Church in 1851, and became Cardinal Archbishop of Westminster in 1865.

It is said that Rottingdean awakened to a great shock in 1928. A new house was being built in the village! Do not imagine from this that Rottingdean is averse to accepting change. Some may remember Volk's Electric Railway which once ran from Rottingdean Pier, (now no more), to Brighton, its cars on stilts alongside the coastline some 50 to 100 yards out to sea. Opened in 1896, it lasted only four years. The greedy sea defeated it, and today, at low tide, all that remains are the concrete pillars that once supported the railway line. The modern version now runs along the shingle from near the Brighton Aquarium at the Palace Pier to Black Rock, its bell sounding a warning for bathers crossing the beach track on their way down to the sea.

Where the last Rottingdean forge stood almost facing the Plough Inn is a block of flats for the elderly. Called Forge House, and completed in 1973, a wall plaque bears witness to the work done in this connection by Mrs. Elizabeth Dacre. The renowned *Black Horse Inn* stands firm in the picturesque High Street against all change, just as it did 500 years ago. Its lounge was once a forge, and some inside walls, built with cow-dung and chalk, are as strong now as when they were built. When the French plundered the village in 1377 on their way to Lewes, helpless villagers were burned to death in St. Margaret's Church tower. There is a horrifying red tint on some of the tower's inside flints to remind us of the ghastly event. More recently, some Americans wanted to buy St. Margaret's and take it over the Atlantic stone by stone. When the attempt failed, they built an exact

Old-world Rottingdean, looking east.

replica in their native land at Glen Dale, California. A hundred years ago, Stephen Welfare, proprietor of the White Horse Hotel, once a notable coaching house on the road to Dover, ran the only bus service to Brighton, carrying the Royal Mail. The dignity of The Grange, now a library and art gallery, houses a famous Toy Museum, whose artist/honorary curator, Yootha Rose, is renowned for her exquisite work. Resident in Brighton, she supervised the Toy Museum. The Trustees of the Toy Museum have presented the entire collection to Brighton Council. Eventually, it may be housed in Northgate House on the Royal Pavilion estate. In the eyes of countless Rottingdean residents and lovers of the ancient village, this proposed removal of the Toy Museum is a great loss to the area. It was founded in the late forties by Leslie Daiken, assisted by Yootha Rose. Responsibility for the collection is now undertaken by Marion Waller, keeper of Preston Manor.

There are indigenous Sussex names of ancient worth in Rottingdean, like Mockford, Dudeney, Snudder, Beard and Copper. Centuries of some families are recorded on mouldering tomb-stones in the graveyard.

There are Rottingdean residents who remember gathering wild orchids on the west-facing Downland rising up behind the village. Today, the orchids no longer exist, and, without sheep, the scrub and gorse are fast creeping across the turf. The same can be said of wheatears, the succulent little birds, described on menus as ortolans, that used to be peculiar to Sussex. In olden times, the best wheatear country was above Rottingdean, and Downland shepherds added considerably to their summer wages by setting snares and netting the birds. During the 17th, 18th, and early part of the 19th centuries, wheatears were taken by shepherds on the Downs in huge quantities and found their way to most of the southern counties' banquets, espe-

114

Victorian shepherd, Rottingdean.

cially during summer, when they were at their plumpest around the time of the wheat. Their name incidentally, meant white tail, and did not indicate that they fed on wheat

In the times of home-made bread around 1870, the women gleaned in the surrounding cornfields, then took their pickings to the windmill for grinding into flour, which was carried home in sacks on their back. Once a miller's child was killed by one of the whirling sails, and a large, rough stone still standing by the mill today is all that remains of the miller's cottage.

At that time, there were no lights in Rottingdean. An oil lamp was put on the centre of the green, but it was moved for the planting of a tree to mark Queen Victoria's jubilee.

Rottingdean's first school was started in the old Vicarage around 1792 by the Rev. T.R. Hooker, and among other famous men who received their early tuition in the village are Sir Stafford Cripps and Lord Bulwer Lytton. The actual village school stood then in the picturesque High Street, known as Rottingdean National, at the foot of the Cowfield, now Nevill Road. When the Nevill Road Houses were built in 1911, they were £250-£300 each, a large sum in those days. The houses known as Victoria Cottages were owned by Mr. George Thomas, whose father was the only man to run the four-horse bus from Rottingdean to Brighton for a 6d. fare. In winter, the bus was made comfortable with straw on the floor. Mr. Thomas, a coal-merchant, sold coal to the villagers at 1s. a bag. In 1603 an inn called *The White Horse and King of Prussia* stood on the site of the present *White Horse* Hotel. During the time of James I (1603-25), the old inn was used as a smugglers'. headquarters. Tradition claims that the smuggled goods were stored in large cellars extending right under the roadway. Bull-baiting, cock-fighting, and other sports of the dissolute Regency bucks, took place there. In cock-fighting, markers used a mahogany chair with a special ledge at the back for their papers. The marker sat straddle-legged on the chair, facing the back. Now very scarce, such chairs today change hands for hundreds of pounds.

AROUND BRIGHTON AND HOVE

The cliffs that form the white, green-topped coastline between Newhaven and Brighton slope gradually to level ground at Brighton's Aquarium, which now boasts a fine Dolphinarium, and the nearby Palace Pier. Westwards is Roedean, a famous public school for girls. Imposingly placed not far from Ovingdean, Roedean was founded in 1885, by the Lawrence sisters. Today, it possesses something unheard of in their strict Victorian era, a head-*master*.

Almost equi-distant east and west from the Royal Sussex County Hospital in Eastern Road stand two of Brighton's other distinguished public schools. Respectively, they are St. Mary's Hall, founded by the Rev. Henry Venn Elliott in 1836 as a boarding school for clergymen's daughters, and Brighton College, founded in 1845 as a publiç school "for the sons of gentlemen, in conformity with the principles of the Established Church". At the opening ceremony of the latter, the Earl of Chichester announced that the new school would diminish "the danger of having a wealthy but uneducated gentry". The total outlay on St. Mary's Hall was £16,000, but, Mr. Elliott, who was the first minister of the present St. Mary and St. James Church in Rock Gardens, helped with finance, land, books and furniture. Queen Adelaide became its first royal patroness. The Marquess of Bristol gave an acre of Downland in the newly-developed Kemp Town, and the architect George Basevi, whom Mr. Elliott met during a tour of Greece, provided the plans for the new school. The original Brighton College Buildings were designed by Sir George Gilbert Scott, later extensions being by an old boy, T.G. Jackson. A far cry from the beginnings of Roedean, known internationally as one of this country's most famous schools. It started in a small way in a house in Kemp Town's lovely Lewes Crescent in 1885, and did not move to its present site until 1899.

From some coast road vantage points, the height of the new tower block of the Royal Sussex County Hospital can be seen rising above

117

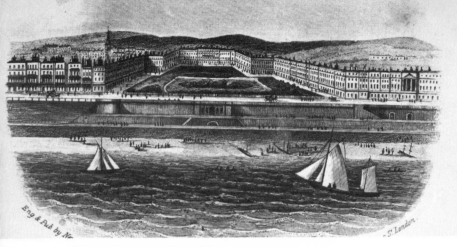

Eighteenth-century Kemp Town.

the Kemp Town area, dwarfing even the Council flats behind at the Kemp Town end of Whitehawk, where prehistoric remains have been unearthed. Gideon Mantell, the great East Sussex geologist, who was born at Lewes in 1790, was reputed to have ground up the fossils he found to make the medicines he used for treating such dreadful diseases as typhus and smallpox. He was the first geologist to point out the fresh-water origin of the Wealden strata, and to him fell the thrilling discovery of enormous dinosaur fossils in that part of East Sussex. From his house at the foot of Castle Keep in Lewes he moved to Brighton, and his geological collections were bought by the British Museum for £4,000.

From pre-history we leap forward to the first exciting pages of an incoming 21st-century Brighton saga. At Black Rock, there is being constructed, both inland and in the sea, what promises to be one of the very finest marinas in Europe, maybe even the world.

What can possibly be said about Brighton, this astounding Regency town, that has not been said a thousand times before? Many people have been judged by their reactions to it. It is princely and prim, vulgar and vain, kind and cruel, wealthy and poor. Those it loves, it applauds, then can forget them overnight. It pities and passes by almost in the same moment. Immensely generous, it can be cannily mean. It is increasingly cosmopolitan, yet sometimes glaringly parochial. Wander through its Royal Pavilion, the Prince Regent's gilded, glorious seaside palace, nurtured by Dr. Clifford Musgrave, former Director of the Royal Pavilion, Museum and Art Gallery.

Cottages in West Street, Mayfield.

The bustling open market on Saturday mornings in Upper Gardner Street, Brighton, is a fantastic voyage of bric-a-brac discovery. Saunter along its ancient Lanes, an antique collector's paradise, study Kemp Town's elegant terraces, crescents and squares which are architectural joys. So are many of the town's centuries-old churches, like Preston Old Church (St. Peter's), one of the most ancient in England and mentioned in Domesday, or St. Nicholas, Brighton's former medieval parish church, where the grave of "Prinny's" famous bathing woman, Martha Gunn, can be seen. The more modern Regency Gothic St. Peter's, which, by an 1870 Order in Council, succeeded St. Nicholas as Brighton's Parish Church, was designed by Sir Charles Barry, and has a beautifully restored ceiling which calls for reflective study. It is an interesting paradox that the gay town so admired by naughty Becky Sharp and Regency bucks was also a place of religious revival!

The two piers are flamboyant, candy-floss meccas for holiday crowds. If you want to see what the butler saw, that's the place to go. The Palace Pier is an ornate, Edwardian silver-coated eye-catcher. On 19th October, 1973, it was severely damaged when a 70-ton barge broke loose from its moorings, and crashed into the supporting piles to the west of the Palace Theatre above, which tipped crazily seawards. Privately owned, the damaged has been estimated at over £100,000, and work on its restoration has begun. Before the Palace Pier existed, Brighton had a Chain Pier. Eventually, it became unsafe, and was finally destroyed in a storm in November 1896.

In Regency days, pebble collecting was a new craze, and in 1835, Oliver Gates, a jeweller and lapidary, opened his shop in Pool Valley. Mr. Gates was always searching for pebbles on the lower part of the shingle near the sand, where the best types could be found. Usually, he was surrounded by ladies in hooped skirts and elegant gallants, all busy in the bracing morning air. His daughter, Mrs. A.T. Nunn, inherited the shop, and often spoke about fishermen who brought in some interesting pebbles caught in their nets. The famous shop, still trading as A.T. Nunn, is today owned by Mrs. May Eldridge, who has worked there for over 40 years.

From around 1770 until the early days of photography, family likenessess were preserved in miniatures and silhouettes. An exciting pursuit in Brighton's early days was to have a silhouette done on the Chain Pier by John Gapp, an artist renowned for his accuracy, and all at 2s 6d. a time for an ordinary one, or 4s. for a likeness picked out in gold! There was an extra charge for framing, and their survival makes silhouettes much more valuable today, especially if there is a

The lychgate cottage, Hartfield.

label pasted on the back with the name of the sitter. The more expensive miniature was also widely commissioned in the county, which was often visited by such great artists as Sir Peter Lely, Sir Godfrey Kneller, Sir Joshua Reynolds and George Romney. They stayed in the stately homes of the Dorsets, the Richmonds, and the Norfolks, where evidence of their works abound. In East Sussex, there are some beautiful examples of Firle Place, of which Baxter produced a fine print in 1826.

The West Pier, one of the oldest in England (1865-66), is also requiring urgent attention because of corrosion. The southern end is, so to speak, sinking below the waves, and specialists in new construction methods have been called in to study the problem. For years Margate jetty was the first example of a successful screw-pile marine construction. The West Pier was modelled on it, others in East Sussex being at Eastbourne and Hastings. In 1868, it achieved sudden notoriety when *The Times* reported panic among promenaders when the structure moved under sea and wind action. The design, in fact, allowed for this, but it caused the pier to become unpopular for a time. A preservation fund has been started by the Regency Society, which, with others, recognises the increasing importance during the next few years, when Brighton will have a large new conference centre nearby. Regarded as the second most architecturally important building in Brighton, the Royal Pavilion being the first, the West Pier is immediately opposite Regency Square, which consists entirely of listed Regency buildings. Let us hope that Brighton's two piers will resume their customary roles, and that, as Patrick O'Donovan said in an article in "The Observer" of 17th March, 1974, we shall again be able to enjoy " . . . that swift walk along the pier, breathing deeply of the cold wind, providing that reasonable measure of discomfort by which the British aquire merit."

The Thomas-Stanford Museum, known as Preston Manor, contains much that is beautiful and absorbing. Its first and second curators contributed greatly to the former home of Sir Charles and Lady Thomas-Stanford, the first being Mr. Henry D. Roberts. He was succeeded by his daughter, who retired in September 1970. The museum was opened on 14th October, 1933, and the Thomas-Stanford Collection of Sussex Deeds was opened by the then Mayor of Brighton, on 14th May, 1953, and can be viewed on application to the present keeper.

Before moving on, let us take one swift, backward glance at Brighton's world-famous Lanes. There, among many treasures, lurks history-packed Black Lion Lane, a narrow twitten, or passage, between the former Black Lion Brewery and the *Cricketers Arms* in Black Lion Street, reputedly the most interesting public house in Brighton from an architectural point of view; late 18th century, it was originally called *The Last and Fish Cart*, a 'last' equalling 10,000 fish. Of all the town's buildings, this inn brings us closest to the great coaching era, when 52 coaches ran daily to and from the then Brighthelmstone. The original brewery was owned by Deryck Carver, the Protestant martyr burned at Lewes in 1554. The later building, recently demolished, was said to have Tudor cellars, and an east front plaque facing Black Lion Street recorded its association with Deryck Carver.

The only building in the Lanes which may be pre-18th century has become two houses in Black Lion Lane, called *Sea Nest* and *The Nook*. The jettied first floor, now slates, probably indicates a 16th-century origin. Mr. Antony Dale, secretary of the Regency Society of Brighton and Hove and renowned for his knowledge of the period, attributes two incidents to Black Lion Lane. The first, perhaps apocryphal, occurred during the escape from England in 1651

122

Friston Church and pond.

of Charles II. He was being carried on a fisherman's back along the passage when a fat fishwife barred their way. Unable to squeeze by, and afraid to retreat, the buxom wench was knocked down to allow the fisherman and monarch to step across her.

The second happened in the 18th century. A well-known athlete was challenged by a fat man to a specified race, with only ten yards start providing the challenger could choose the track. The latter selected Black Lion Lane. Narrow enough for his bulk nearly to touch each wall, this enabled him to cover the distance without his opponent being able to pass him.

Brighton, alias 'London by the Sea', has racing at the Race Hill Racecourse with its fabulous views, the Brighton and Hove Albion Football Club and Brighton Rugby Club, while Hove draws the crowds to the green leisure of its well-sited County Cricket Ground and the competitive thrills of its Greyhound Stadium. The Downs just behind Brighton provide a magnificent site for a race-course, and the town's first races were held in August 1783. Today, the downhill run is considered one of the fastest in the country. The course, like Epsom's, is horse-shoe shaped. From about 1760, meetings at Lewes, whose races were older than Brighton's, had been attended by the gentry and nobility staying at Brighton, and their increasing numbers made it essential for a seaside course to be established. After the Prince Regent attended Brighton races in 1784, they became ever more important. In 1875 they emerged as a leading social event lasting four days, and a year before the stand was erected in 1788, 'Prinny' and Mrs. Fitzherbert attended with such notables as the Duke and Duchess of Richmond, the Dukes of Bedford and Queensberry, Lords Abergavenny, Egremont and Grosvenor, and Mr. Charles James Fox. In 1787, the Prince stayed in the town for over three months, when "the company" was stated to be "double that of any previous year". Writing in 1799 in his *The Balnea: or an impartial Description of all Popular Watering Places in England'*, G.S. Carey remarked: "Brighton has less diversity than Margate, and less tranquillity than Tunbridge Wells, but I believe it is visited by more nobility than either of the foregoing places. This may proceed from the Heir Apparent making it his summer residence, for the eagles and hawks for ever gather round the highest rocks."

Brighton, beloved by Thackeray, who called it "Kind, merry, cheerful Dr. Brighton!", also boasts a world-famous Aquarium and Dolphinarium. The Aquarium was established as a private company in 1869, opened in 1871, and with the West Pier (1866) proved a rival of the Chain Pier, described by the Victorians as an "elegant Wonder

St. Dunstan's, Ian Fraser House, Ovingdean, Near Brighton.

of Science". In its early days of phenomenal success, Edward VII, Queen Alexandra and many European monarchs "toured the tanks". Designed by Mr. E. Birch of London, mainly in the Italian style, it took three years to build, and has unique arched corridors, rock-framed tanks and huge subterranean storage tanks for sea water. Brighton Corporation acquired it in 1900. Alterations were made both at that time, and again in 1927, when it was modernised at a cost of around £136,000, the statues of the old Aquarium being removed to gardens at Patcham. In 1956, the building reverted to private enterprise.

In 1968 a major scheme costing £200,000 resulted in a new pool 80 feet by 30 feet and 10 feet in depth. Special filtration maintains 200,000 gallons of sea water at around 72° Fahrenheit. Apart from an exotic variety of fishes, turtles and penguins, there are six delightful dolphins named Belle, Prinny, Missus, Baby, Lucky and Poppy, the last being a tribute to a former Mayoress of Brighton. The two seals are Sunshine and her boy-friend, Yogi, and there is a family of 10 sea lions, the largest in the country.

Hove, on the other hand, has the aquatic and social amenities of the King Alfred Pool, where the local branch of the British Sub-Aqua Club, the biggest in the world with a membership of 25,000, trains weekly. Brighton is regarded as a pioneer in the sport, one of the world's boom leisure activities, which is also practised at the very latest Newhaven-Seaford branch. When the Brighton branch was formed in 1954, there were only seven members. Today, it has 450, and is growing constantly. The King Alfred Sports Centre in Hove also now boasts the new Sussex Ice Club, founded by ice-skating star Valerie Moon and Mr. William Burn, a refrigeration ice engineer and former skater, who built and supplied the Hove rink. It is interesting to note that this East Sussex amenity, so much needed after the closure of the Brighton ice rink, came into being 100 years after the first private one was opened in Chelsea in 1876.

Brighton has the fountain-graced Old Steine, a Scandinavian word which means 'Stone'. Through it ran a stream called the Wellsbourne, with its source at Patcham and outflow into the sea in Pool Valley, where, on the west side, stands Cowley's celebrated *Bunne Shoppe*, built in 1794 and still owned by descendants of the original family. Faced with black mathematical tiles, it retains the original front, complete with glazing bars. Hove, on the other hand, has the splended sweep along Grand Avenue from the sea front, across Church Road, then up the Drive, where Hove Parish Church, All Saints, is a magnificent edifice that causes grave concern through stone deterioration. Marlborough House in Brighton's Steine, and probably the most important house in the town, is now the Information Office. It was built for the Duke of Marlborough in 1769. He sold it in 1786 to William Gerald Hamilton, M.P., better known as "single-speech" Hamilton, who employed Robert Adam to erect the present house. Steine House next door, once Mrs. Fitzherbert's home, is the Brighton headquarters of the Y.M.C.A., who refaced it entirely when they took it over in 1884. Originally, it had a rather rustic appearance with trellised verandah and balcony. Most of its interior features remain, including the cast-iron imitation bamboo staircase up which the Earl of Barrymore once rode a horse for a bet. It was linked by a passage to the King's bedroom in the Royal Pavilion.

Brighton's claim to hotel fame probably rests quite securely on the Royal Albion, erected on the site where stood the former Russell House, built for his own use in 1754 by the celebrated, toothless Dr. Richard Russell, whose "sea-water is beneficial" advice founded Brighton's fame and fortune. The Albion Hotel was built in 1826, the word 'Royal' being added later because of the number of distinguished visitors who stayed there.

Brighton's museum and art gallery are notable, one of whose latest outstanding acquisitions is the painting by Francis Wheatley, R.A., of 'The Encampment at Brighton', bought for the art gallery in the autumn of 1973 for £24,000. Brooker Hall at Hove is also noteworthy as a museum. Its treasures had to be stored away suddenly just after 9th January, 1966, when the borough's well-loved Victorian Gothic Town Hall was virtually destroyed by a calamitous fire. From then, until Brooker Hall reopened as a museum on 22nd March 1974, it became the then Borough Council's headquarters. Today, Hove has a new Town Hall, designed by architect John Wells-Thorpe, who said of the glass-and-concrete civic centre, that it was meant to take the "stuffed shirt atmosphere" out of civic architecture. Despite some customary criticisms, this appears to have been achieved.

At Sussex University in Stanmer Park, can be seen the Chichester family's Stanmer Church, a lovely visual gem, now 136 years old, and Sussex University is proud of the artistic achievements of its Gardner Theatre Centre. The University also owns 18th-century Stanmer House, once the home of the Earls of Chichester, built for Henry and Thomas Pelham, and very important as it is the only known complete English work of the architect, Nicholas Dubois.

Nearby Falmer village originally belonged to the Chichesters. Today, its south side has belonged to Brighton Corporation for over 26 years, the north side being sold around 1960 to the university. East of St. Laurence Church, in Norman style but of Victorian vintage, lies a farm that possesses a splendid tithe barn with a marvellous timber roof. Local people say it is much older than the

Lewes Crescent, Kemp Town, Brighton — a fine example of Regency Architecture.

attributed 16th century. Like Pyecombe and Kingston, near Lewes, shepherds' crooks were made at Falmer in days when the Downs were thick with sheep. In 1959, Falmer Post Office-cum-grocery-cum-off-licence was featured in a colourful poster issued in connection with the Post Office Savings Bank campaign, based on a painting by Michael Manning. The living room fireplace has deep cupboards on either side, and a chimney in which an original spit chain was discovered by a sweep. Another exciting 'find' was in the big cellar; carriage candles and blacking in large Victorian stone jars.

Three of the greatest projects that have emerged in Brighton during the past decade are its annual international festivals of the arts, the now-emerging Brighton Centre on the sea front between the piers, and the gigantic Brighton Marina project at Black Rock. Before 1967, when the first Brighton Festival of the Arts was held from 14th to 30th April, the late Lord Cohen of Brighton was actively connected with its inception.

The Music and Banqueting Rooms at the Royal Pavilion are the regal settings for many festival and other varied local occasions. The King William IV room is one of those used for classes in Brighton's annual Competitive Musical Festival, which celebrated its Golden Jubilee in 1974.

Cottages at East Dean.

The Royal Pavilion, Brighton.

On 1st November, 1975, the Music Room was set on fire by petrol thrown by a 22-year-old art student. Built in 1818, renovation has been continuous since the 1940s. King George IV sang for his guests in the Music Rooms, where some of the ornate carvings can never be properly replaced. It was once described as the "most beautiful room in the world". The winged dragons and serpents are considered quite irreplaceable.

In April 1977, insurance totalling £225,000 was agreed in respect of the Music Room. Restoration will not be completed until 1982, a task described as one of the most complicated ever undertaken.

The original house was built in 1786-87 by Henry Holland for George IV when Prince of Wales. Simple and classical, it was known as the Marine Pavilion of His Royal Highness, a name that has survived all subsequent changes. In 1801-3, it was enlarged and given its first Chinese interior. The Prince then commissioned William Porden to build the stables and riding house to the west, known as the Dome and Corn Exchange. Constructed in Hindu style, the stables gave the Prince the idea of orientalising the outside of his seaside residence. Between 1815 and 1820, John Nash, architect of the

Regent's Park terraces in Marylebone, wrought the changes we see today.

Without doubt one of the most remarkable buildings in the country, the Royal Pavilion has been adulated and scorned. William Hazlitt called it "a collection of stone pumpkins and pepper boxes". William Cobbett, who, according to *Chambers Encyclopedia*, Vol, 3, p.694, Col.A, wrote under the pseudonym of 'Peter Porcupine', thought it was like a "parcel of 'cradle spits', of various dimensions, sticking up out of the mouths of so many enormous squat decanters", or "a series of turnips and flower bulbs placed on top of a square box". Charles Molloy Westmacott likened it to the ornaments on a dinner table. He wrote: "The central dome represents the water magnum, the towers right and left, with their pointed spires, champagne bottles, the square compartments on each side are exactly like the form of our fashionable 'liquer' stands". Some said it looked like chessmen set on a board. The most famous gibe was Sydney Smith's who declared that "the dome of St. Paul's must have come down to Brighton and pupped". Much of this was due to Whig reaction against the Prince, who turned Tory after becoming Regent. Cobbett and others regarded the Pavilion as a reactionary hotbed, and satirically called it "the Kremlin". For those who revel in its erotic sumptuousness, Brighton's royal home is above reproach. In these high materialistic days, it has become a money-spinner *par excellence*. Foresight and dedication to its preservation and improvement have paid fantastic dividends, not only for Brighton but "the world and his wife" who visit this Regency resort in countless thousands.

Brighton's next architectural glories are found in Kemp Town, Turn eastwards from the Steine along what was originally the Brighton to Rottingdean turnpike road, and you will find magnificent crescents and terraces. Royal Crescent, faced with black mathematical tiles, was built between 1799 and 1807 by West Indian speculator, J.B. Otto, and an unknown architect. Originally, a buff-coloured plaster statue of the Prince, dressed as a Colonel of the 10th Hussars, stood 7ft. high on an 11ft. pedestal. Frequently mistaken for Lord Nelson, its damaged remains were removed in 1819. Mrs. Fitzherbert is buried in nearby St. John the Baptist Roman Catholic Church. Designed by Carew, her tomb on the east wall shows the three wedding rings of her three marriages, including that to George IV, then Prince of Wales.

George Canning, Foreign Minister from 1822-27 and Prime Minister for a few months before his death in 1827, had a house on the pres-

The Palace Pier, Brighton.

ent Marine Parade site of the Royal Crescent Hotel. Marine Square was built about 1824, and was laid out by a local solicitor called Thomas Attree, who also built himself a fine Villa in Queen's Park, occupied at a later date by the Xaverian College and other schools, and now demolished. The Palladian-fronted former Royal German Spa and Pump Room in the park has had a chequered career since it was built in 1824-5, south of a park named after Queen Adelaide, at a cost of £2,506, by Cooper and Lyon. Mr. Loraine is presumed to have been its architect. Doctor F.A.A. Struve, of Dresden and the famous artificial mineral waters firm bearing his name, opened it in June, 1825, as a German Spa. George IV gave it his patronage, hence its subsequent title of Royal German Spa, now simply the Royal Spa. In a state of decay, its future is still uncertain.

Collingwood House at the south-east corner of Marine Square originally had a fine staircase, now spoiled by the insertion of a lift in its well. Next, Portland Place was the last work in Brighton of Charles Augustus Busby. His design for it was exhibited in 1830 in the Royal Academy. He also designed the Royal Church of St. George nearby. Built in 1824 as the chapel of Ease for Kemp Town, the interior has galleries of the period, and also the royal pew. Seymour Street has been swept away for pseudo-Regency house development, and the L-shaped Eastern Terrace, built around 1828, has

131

formal houses, with extra balconies added on the second floor of one, and very fine staircases. That in No. 1 is probably the most remarkable in the town, again marred by a lift. The frontage is so curved that the main rooms on ground and first floors are almost circular. From 1876 to 1896, it was occupied by Sir Albert Sassoon, first member of the family to live in England. He built himself a mausoleum at the north-east corner of Paston Place, now a convivial rendezvous called the Bombay Bar. He was buried there in 1896, also his son, Sir Edward, in 1912. Their remains were removed by Sir Albert's grandson, Sir Philip, when the latter sold the fantastic property in 1933. The family had a riding school on the site of the Odeon Cinema, now used as a bingo hall. The Shah of Persia was entertained at No. 1 Eastern Terrace for several days in 1889, and Edward VII, when Prince of Wales, lunched there in 1881 and 1896. King Manoel of Portugal occupied No. 9 during part of his exile in England.

The great builder, Thomas Cubitt, built Belgrave Place in 1846, also Eaton Place. Philosopher Herbert Spencer lived further east in Percival Terrace, named after its builder, W. Percival Boxall, who built it between 1845-50. Chichester Terrace, roughly contemporary with Clarendon Terrace, is in Kemp Town proper, whose main gems are also Lewes Crescent and Arundel Terrace leading to Black Rock.

Projected in 1823, by Thomas Read Kemp, a joint Lord of the Manor of Brighton and owner of most open East Cliff land, the

George IV's bedroom in the Royal Pavilion.

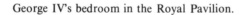

Kemp Town estate was originally meant to be twice its present size. Because lack of adequate funds caused it to stand away from the town at first, it was called Kemp Town as it was not part of Brighton. Today, the words Kemp Town are used to cover a large postal area extending west to the Old Steine. Originally, it meant only Chichester Terrace, Lewes Crescent, Sussex Square and Arundel Terrace. Because different architects were chosen by Kemp, also different builders, no two houses are identical, even in original construction. Cubitt built 37 of the 106 houses. The garden enclosure was laid out for Thomas Read Kemp by a local botanist, Henry Phillips. The series of slopes and esplanades were built for private use. The slopes, now in public use, hold great interest as they are the only portion of Brighton's sea front still virtually intact as designed in 1830. Beneath the cliff, they were connected with the main garden above by a tunnel under the Rottingdean turnpike road. The esplanades included two gardeners' cottages flanking the entrance to a tunnel on the upper terrace and a lower room used as a reading room.

From 1853 to 1867, Harrison Ainsworth lived at 5, Arundel Terrace, Brighton, where he lavishly entertained friends who "used to walk from the Station along the sea front to his home." The five-storey, pillared residence was bought in 1956 by Madame Julie de Belleroche, who lived just outside Paris, and whose renowned artist husband Albert de Belleroche, died just before the end of the Second World War. One of her sons was Count William de Belleroche, equally well-known as an artist and exotic personality of Brighton. He lived at the Arundel Terrace house from 1956 until his death in March, 1969. He also owned Pulborough Manor in West Sussex for a short time, and people still talk about the Elizabethan Ball he organised there not long before his death. His sister, Alice Sutton, the classical guitarist, regularly visits Brighton from her home in Paris.

The boundary between Brighton and Hove lies between Western Street and Waterloo Street. On the front it is marked by the Peace Memorial, built in 1912 in memory of King Edward VII, who used to enjoy sitting in a shelter on the promenade when on his frequent visits to Brighton. The monument stands half in Brighton and half in Hove. Vast blocks of flats have merged along the sea front, such as Sussex Heights and Bedford Towers, the latter containing the home of Lady Cohen of Brighton.

Like Kemp Town, Brunswick Square was meant to be self-supporting. Brunswick Terrace was built about the same time, between 1825 and 1830, and they were at first jointly called 'Brunswick Town'. The Brunswick Square Act of 1830 was one of the last Acts of

Regency Square, Brighton.

Parliament passed in the reign of George IV. This set up a special body called the Brunswick Square commissioners, who regulated all matters in the 'new town' of Hove. After Kemp Town, this square and terrace are the most important architectural features in Brighton and Hove. Recently, it was revealed that Brunswick Terrace is now in a serious condition, and presents an enormous case for conservation. The buildings are largely empty due to lamented deterioration, and Hove Council are considering conservation either in the form of continued use for housing or for commercial purposes. Like the West Pier, this presents major financial problems. Adelaide Crescent was the third of the important estates built in the reigns of George IV and William IV. Laid out in 1830, it was first called Queen Adelaide Crescent as a compliment to the new Queen. The architect was Decimus Burton, then working for his father, James Burton, in the construction of the new St. Leonards-on-Sea near Hastings.

When Sussex music-lovers think of Brighton, they think of Brighton Philharmonic Orchestra, founded in 1925 by the late musical director Herbert Menges, who conducted his last concert on 13th February, 1972, and died suddenly a week later. A plaque to his memory hangs in the foyer of the Dome, where he conducted 326 concerts. Menges changed the face of Brighton, described by composer-conductor Sir Landon Ronald as a 'musical desert'. His mother, Madame Kate Menges, took the first bold steps when she formed the Symphonic String Players, whose stated aim was "to become a large and powerful orchestra, and to give periodical concerts of a high standard in Brighton and Hove". Her son, Herbert, conducted, with the late Molly Paley as leader. The Society's first concert on 18th May, 1925, opened in the old Hove Town Hall with Tchaikovsky's Serenade, Op. 48. Today, the town is packed with music and musical societies.

The Young Phil, whose chairman is Ian Wallace, is a separate organisation, yet linked through the society. Brighton Youth Orchestra is now internationally renowned, having been founded after the second World War through the initiative of Ronald Harding, former first cellist of the London Symphony Orchestra and, for a time, conductor of the National Youth Orchestra of Wales. He was succeeded for a period by Wilfred Smith before David Gray assumed control.

Drama in East Sussex is splendidly represented by a number of fine theatres, including the civic, multi-purpose hall Congress Theatre in Eastbourne, with its 1,678 two-tier seats, built on the edge of Devonshire Park in 1963, and a noteworthy successor to the Winter Garden which had been on the same site since 1874. Further east,

135

there are the Devonshire Park Theatre at Bexhill, built with two Italianate towers in 1884, and, of course, the De La Warr Pavilion, built between 1933 and 1936, and used much more often for musical events. Hastings has its White Rock Pavilion. There, comedian Jack Tripp in the Fol-De-Rols' summer shows was to Hastings what another famous comedian, Max Miller, an ever-popular figure in Jack Sheppard's show facing the sea front lift in Kemp Town, was to Brighton. Hastings also has its estimable Stables Theatre, opened in the High Street in 1959 by Sir Ralph Richardson. Almost 250 years old, the building is a fine example of domestic Georgian architecture. Its picturesque site is at the historic entrance to the Cinque Port in the valley between East and West Hill and almost opposite the 15th-century church. Originally built as stabling in 1746 for John Collier, five times Mayor of Hastings, it was used for billets for his Brigade troops when the Duke of Wellington was stationed in the town during the Napoleonic wars.

In Brighton, the Theatre Royal takes precedence over all. The property's original conveyance bears the signature of the Prince of Wales, and it opened in June, 1807, under the Prince Regent's patronage, with an appearance of Mr. and Mrs. Charles Kemble as Hamlet and Ophelia. The entire cost was £12,000, and the early days were marked by some financial difficulties, including the high cost of such stars as Sarah Siddons, Grimaldi, Charles Kean, Ellen Terry, Sarah Bernhardt, Julia Neilson, Martin Harvey, Seymour Hicks, Henry Irving, Fred Terry, Weedon Grossmith, Mrs. Patrick Campbell, Madame Vestris, and others far too numerous to mention. In 1826, the elegant bow windows and colonnade were added, the former on the first floor now giving a fine view of the Royal Pavilion from the dress circle bar.

The Gardner Theatre Centre at Sussex University is in lovely Stanmer Park, and sparkles with youthful vigour and talent. The design emerged from the unification of the arts in a circular building with surrounding studios for painting, music and sculpture. The Gardner Centre is an East Sussex arts dream which provides the county with a rare building where opera, music, drama, folk singing, ballet and art exhibitions can all be accommodated by merely adapting the interior. It is an East Sussex free-for-all that encompasses every aspect of social and artistic life.

10

THE PIONEERS

East Sussex can claim pioneers in many fields. Among these must be included William Friese-Green, (1855-1921) for cinematography, a name of such international fame as to need no further embellishment here. Magnus Volk (1851-1937), a pioneer in electricity, who planned and built at Brighton the first electric railway in Great Britain, affectionately known as "Daddy-long-legs", and whose house was the first in Brighton to be lit by electricity, and, lastly, John Saxby for railways. After learning to be a joiner and carpenter, Saxby joined the Brighton and South Coast Railway, started in 1852, became a pattern-maker and, eventually, foreman in one of the shops. Concerned with safety in signalling, he patented a signal lamp. In 1856, he took out patent No. 1479, generally regarded as the beginning of interlocking between points and signals. Further patents came along in 1858 and 1860. It is believed he may have started the first production of signalling equipment in Sussex around 1860. He lived, with a family of five, in Buckingham Road, former venue of Brighton Maternity Hospital, now housed in the new block at the Royal Sussex County Hospital in Kemp Town.

John Saxby's story ties up, somehow, with the old Brighton and Dyke Railway that ran from Aldrington Halt to a station in the valley near Devil's Dyke. The buildings can still be seen easily from the top of a bus, the old station being where a farm now stands as one approaches a fork in the road just before the Dyke. The old track can be seen easily on a Brighton-Hove map. It passed under the Old Shoreham Road and beside Elm Drive and Rowan Avenue, where there was a station called Rowan Halt. Then it passed between the present Dale View and Popular Avenue, and emerged into the valley in the Downs beside Brighton and Hove golf course. An independent railway, it became part of the Southern Railway in 1924, which had to pay all its debts, and ran until closure just before the Second World War.

137

Hove's new Town Hall.

Brighton and Hove High School for Girls recalls Thomas Read Kemp. Once known as The Temple, from which Temple Gardens takes its name, he built it for himself in flamboyant style and to proportions said to approximate those in King Solomon's temple. In 1827 it was auctioned without success, and again in 1842. These abortive events may have been connected with its name of "Kemp Folly", or because its dome-topped, flat roofed creation was linked with a strange religious sect he founded. Most of its outrageous features have now been removed.

In Brighton Parish Register we find the following item: "*The fourteenth day of this month King Charles the Second went from this towne out of Mr. Smith's house and was taken aboard by Nic Tetersoale and conveyed to France*". The name Tetersoale is spelt in differing ways, such as Tettershall, Tettershell, Tettersfield or Tettersell. It is, however, always the same 'Nic', for Nicholas, who entered our history books so suddenly in October 1651, six weeks after the Battle of Worcester and the flight from Boscobel. The tombstone of the former coal brig captain can be seen on the south side of St. Nicholas churchyard, Brighton, the name there being Tettersell. While some ask if he was Brightelmstone man, he certainly lived in the town in 1651, when having managed to get the 21-year old monarch fugitive, who had £1,000 on his head, safely on his coal boat at Shoreham at low tide, he raced back home to Brighton to get some "necessities", and kiss his wife goodbye before setting off on his memorable cross-Channel trip. Years later, he retired and became Brighton's chief public official. One-time landlord of the *Old Ship Hotel*, and High Constable in 1670, when he enforced the stern Carolean measures against Quakers and non-comformists, he married a second time early in 1694 and died on 26th July in the same year.

A little way east of Tettersell's tomb lies that of the Prince Regent's celebrated bathing woman, or 'dipper', Martha Gunn, with her husband and four children. Born in 1762, she lived to be 89, probably a tribute to her adherence to Doctor Russell's injunction about sea bathing. One of "Prinny's" favourites, she often visited the kitchens in the Royal Pavilion, and, not being averse to royal perks, it is recorded that on one occasion when he entered the kitchen, the Prince noticed her slip a pound of butter into her pocket. Cunningly edging her way around the stone-flagged place, he kept her talking in front of the big fireplace. The resultant pool of butter at her feet revealed the sorry truth! Fortunately, "Prinny" was not known for bearing malice, so the tale had a happy ending.

While on the subject of bathing, it must be remembered that if our inland spas imitated the Bath of Beau Nash, Brighton modelled itself, in Martha Gunn's day, on Tunbridge Wells, even following its custom of welcoming new arrivals "for the waters" with a peal of bells. It is recorded that in 1782, Brighton bells were "set a-ringing for the arrival of Lord and Lady Fitzwilliam".

Dr. Russell, whose main peculiarity was that he made his patients drink the sea-water as well as bathe in it, certainly instigated the sea-side mania. As George Roberts stated, "he was to seaside visitors what Peter the Hermit was to the crusades — the genius that raised the latent spirit".

Another famous Brighton woman, whose fame outshone even that of Martha Gunn, is Phoebe Hassell, born in 1713 during Queen Anne's reign. For 17 years she served with the King's colours, not as a vivaniere, fairly common in those days, but as an ordinary soldier. At 15, she fell in love with a soldier called Golding. When his regiment was ordered overseas, Phoebe enlisted in another regiment bound for the West Indies. During all her service, she managed to preserve her secret, even when her arm was wounded at the Battle of Fontenoy in 1745. When her lover was wounded and invalided home, she told her secret to her regimental colonel, and was granted a discharge. The two lovers married and lived happily for 20 years until his death, after which she settled in Brighton, married a man named Hassell, and survived him. When she died, aged 108, she was the town's oldest inhabitant, and during her last years received a weekly pension of 10s from George IV.

Three other interesting tombs in St. Nicholas's churchyard deserve a mention. The first, to the east of the church is that of the well known 19th-century actress, Maria Crouch, whose tombstone is surmounted by a large urn, and whose unusual epitaph is worth recording:-

She combined with the purest taste as a singer
the most elegant simplicity as an Actress
beautiful almost beyond parallel in her Person.
She was distinguished by the powers of her mind
they enabled her when she had quitted the stage
to gladden the life by the charms of her
conversation and refine it by her manners.

At the churchyard's lower east end is a large tomb topped by a shell ornament on what is an outstanding monument. It is to Amon Wilds, one of three architects responsible for the finest Regency squares in Brighton and Hove. His architect son, Amon Henry Wilds, probably designed the tomb because he often used shell motifs on the façades of Brighton houses he designed. No longer legible, his tomb inscription also deserves recording:-

"A remarkable incident accompanies the period at which this gentleman came to settle in Brighton. Through his abilities and taste, the order of the ancient architecture of buildings in Brighton may be dated to have changed from its antiquated simplicity and rusticity; and its improvements have since progressively increased. He was a man of extensive genius, and talent, and his reputation for uprightness of conduct could only meet its parallel".

North of the church lies another centenarian, Sake Deen Mahomed, who first introduced Turkish baths into England. After service as a surgeon in the Indian Army, he came to East Sussex, and in Brighton opened some vapour baths, or shampooing, as it was then known. Reputed to be good for rheumatism, Mahomed decorated his premises with his cured patients' crutches! He was appointed Shampooing Surgeon to George IV, and died at 102 in 1851.

Sir John Gibney, an Edinburgh graduate who became senior physician to the Sussex County Hospital and General Sea-bathing infirmary in Brighton, sent patients to Mahomed, and wrote two short books on bathing. The first appeared in 1813, and was called "*Practical Observation on the Use and Abuse of Cold and Warm Sea-Bathing in various diseases, particularly in Scrofulous and Gouty cases"*. The second, published in 1825, was *"A Treatise on the Properties and Medical Application of the Vapour Bath"*. It appeared when vapour baths had become more popular, largely as the result of Sake Deen Mahomed's work.

St. Nicholas Church itself excited an un-named poet in 1796 to pen lines to its former weather vane, mistakenly described as a shark. Today, with a famous sextet of dolphins in the town, it is good to know that one of these intelligent mammals graced the then Parish Church. It is equally sad to reflect that many consider the penultimate line of this quoted verse is a perfect description of modern Brighton. It reads:-

> *"Say why on Brighton's Church we see*
> *a golden shark displayed,*
> *But that 't'was aptly meant to be*
> *An emblem of its trade?*
> *Nor could the things so well be told*
> *In any other way --*
> *A town's a shark that lives on gold,*
> *The company its prey"*

Henry Pratt, watch-maker and clock-maker, lived in Preston Street, which is currently suffering loss of trade through traffic changes in Brighton, and is not far from the new *Bedford Hotel*, built after the old Ionic one (where Charles Dickens loved to stay) was burnt down on April 1st, 1964. It was designed by Thomas Cooper, architect of Brighton Town Hall. The new *Bedford Hotel* was opened on September 16th, 1967. A remarkable Brightonian, Thomas Cooper was born on March 29th, 1838, and became an amateur astronomer of note. He is remembered as the constructor of the gilded turret clock in the former Congregational Church at the Dials, Brighton. The sad task of demolishing its prominent landmark tower began on the 26th April, 1972, and the entire building was razed before the end of the year. His other noted local clock was given to the then Brighton Workhouse, now Brighton General Hospital, in 1874.

Henry Pratt's father, another Henry, was a noted naturalist and taxidermist. With his other sons and grandsons, he was responsible for many of the exhibits in the present Booth Museum of Natural History in Dyke Road, Brighton. Established as a private museum in 1874 by Mr. E.T. Booth, every bird fell to his own gun. On his death in 1890, the now-famous museum was taken over by Brighton Corporation and functions under the aegis of the County Borough's Art

141

The Sackville memorial in Withyham Church.

Gallery and Museums and the Royal Pavilion, directed by John Morely, who began his duties in September 1968.

From 1890, various collections were bought, and further ranges of cases built to included some of the rarer Sussex species. One of the most important in the world, the museum contains specimens of the majority of species known to have inhabited or visited these islands. A number of cases are devoted to illustrating seasonal variations in plumage. The Booth Museum also houses the complete natural history collections of the Brighton museums, including thousands of insects, foreign birds, mammals and extensive geological collections.

One of the county's most famous botanists was William Borrer, born in 1781. His knowledge of Sussex plant life has probably never been equalled. A present-day personality who has spent much of his spare time studying plant life in East Sussex is the Rev. Thomas Glaisyer whose great-great-grandfather founded Glaisyer and Kemp in 1790, the well known chemist's shop in Brighton's Castle Square.

Moving west past the building site of the new Brighton Centre, the Hotel Metropole and its massive complex of conference halls, with Sussex Heights towering aloft, and the lesser yet no less imposing structure of Bedford Towers above the Bedford Hotel, one must not forget, as many do, the little French Church, tucked away unassumingly behind the Hotel Metropole. It was established by the Huguenots off Regency Square, and came into being in the 16th century when a few French Protestants escaped to England from religious persecution and settled in the then fishing village of Brightelmstone. Some Norman and Flemish people were already there, so services in French were held by the newcomers in their homes, notably in the house of Derick Carver, who lived in Black Lion Street, where the site can still be seen. Here, English and French Protestants joined forces and built a United Church. Union Street takes its name from that amalgamation of the two nations in religious worship.

During those troubled times. Elizabth I protected her Protestant subjects by providing Brighton with six pieces of heavy artillery. Erected in Gun Gardens, between Black Lion Street and East Street, the blockhouse walls were 8-feet thick and 18-feet high! After the horrors of St. Bartholomew's Day, the French Church in Brighton received and succoured thousands of refugees from France. They joined it, and in 1875 a ten-day convention was held in the town, with 200 Pastors and 8,000 visitors from the Continent taking part. On one day during the event, a prayer meeting was planned in the Corn Exchange. By 6.30 in the morning, the building was crammed to the doors!

Aerial view of Sussex University with Brighton in the distance.

On 24th May, 1959, the little church celebrated the founding of the first Synod of the Reformed Church of France, and the founding of the College of Geneva by Jean Calvin.

The coming of the railway caused many churches to be built in Brighton, no less than 13 Anglican ones being added to the existing 14 between 1841 and 1875. The Wagners, father and son, were the great church builders, the elder, Henry Michell Wagner, Vicar of Brighton from 1824-70, being noted as having built St. Paul's with its soaring tower in West Street at his own expense! His son, Arthur Douglas Wagner, was its first vicar, and its treasures included the altarpiece behind the high altar, and early work of Burne-Jones and Pugin windows. Its architect was R.C. Carpenter, "next to Butterfield the greatest of the Tractarian architects", who also designed All Saint's in Compton Avenue. The Chapel Royal in New Road was used by the Prince Regent, who ceased to worship there after being criticised from the pulpit. The Unitarian Church, with its noble Doric portico, and built in 1820 to designs by A.H. Wilds, was regarded as superior to most others at that time. The younger

Wagner built four churches at his own expense, including St. Bartholomew's in Ann Street. Opened in 1874, it cost £17,000 to build, the architect being Edmund Scott. Called "Noah's Ark" by its denigrators, or "Wagner's Folly", in much the same way the Royal Pavilion was dubbed "Florizel's Folly", it has been described as "one of the most remarkable buildings in the British Isles" because of its severe design and great height of 135 feet. People living in houses adjacent to its west wall complained that its height created a severe down-draught, and made their chimneys "smoke intolerably". Mr Wagner bought up all their properties, then reduced the rents! He also built, among much else, some 400 working-class houses in the Lewes Road area. The present Wagner Hall in Brighton, opened on 30th June, 1972, is named in memory of Arthur Wagner. Owned and administered by St. Paul's, it was opened by Sir Anthony Wagner, a descendant, and present Garter Principal King of Arms. St. Stephen's church has a strange history worth recording. When the old *Castle Inn* was pulled down in 1819 to make way for an extension to the Royal Pavilion, its splended 18th-century ballroom was converted into a Royal Chapel. After the purchase of the Pavilion estate by the Town Commissioner, the chapel was moved bodily to a site in Montpelier Place in 1851, and renamed St. Stephen's. St. Ann's

Duckings, Withyham.

Church, in Burlington Street, was given to Kemp Town in 1861, and St. Michael's deserves a mention for its Morris and Rosetti stained glass.

Apart from the Royal Pavilion and 'Kemp's Folly', in Montpelier Road, one further exotic building still remains. Some ten years after the latter building was built, a banker and horticultural expert called Henry Phillips, dreamed up a piece of fantastic town-planning for Hove which he said would be called Oriental Place, which, in fact, is all that remains today of the grandiose scheme. This envisaged the Royal Pavilion motifs included in buildings surrounding a huge rectangular plot of land laid out as a superlative garden. It was described in the then "*Brighton Gazette*" in these words:- "The idea we can give of the appearance which the grove will present is by comparing it to the cemetery of Pere La Chaise or to the city of Constantinople with its roofs and minarets embowered by trees". Only one short terrace of three houses was completed, together with the Antheum, a huge, glass dome covering an acre and a half of ground. The framework was cast-iron, and the enormous conservatory was 160 feet wide and 54 feet high. Inside, it was laid out with gravel walks and tropical and European trees and plants. It was a fore-runner of the Crystal Palace, and its dome was larger that that of St. Peter's, Rome, and the largest plant-house in existence at the time.

Henry Phillips started to build the Antheum early in 1833 on land, and with money belonging to financier Isaac Lyon Goldsmid, who became the first Jewish baronet, and later, Lord Palmeira. Before the building was completed, the architect, Amon Henry Wilde, grew so apprehensive about stability that he withdrew from the project. His place was taken by C. Hollis, and his place as contractor by English, who, on the day before it opened on 29th August, 1833, pulled away the main shoring which had supported the building. A few hours after the opening ceremony, the entire structure fell to pieces, leaving a tangled mass of broken glass and iron girders which was not removed from the site for some years. As no one was present, no injury resulted, but Henry Phillips was so devastated that he went blind from shock. The site of The Antheum is now Palmeria Square, and the rest of the proposed Oriental Place has been succeeded by beautiful Adelaide Crescent and Square.

West from Adelaide Crescent, once called "Royal" as a gesture to the new Queen, the architecture changes. The architectural dignity of the early 19th century ends, and from here on there is little to enchant, and much to decry. One can say that Hove's wide and well-planned roads leading down to the sea are admirable, especially in

Firle Place, built in the 16th century.

these days of parking problems. Good examples of their kind, many of Hove's avenues were built by Sir James Knowles, an architect who turned journalist and became editor of the "*Nineteeth Century*" magazine. Hove Street was the site of the original village of Hove, which remained one until well into the 19th century, and the fine 18th-century Manor House, sited half-way up the east side, was unfortunately demolished in 1936. There are some fine churches in the area, the interior of Hove Parish Church, All Saints' being probably one of the finest 19th-century Gothic examples in England.

West Blatchington and Hangleton are modern suburbia, but were village settlements originally. St. Helen's church at Hangleton is, like St. Lawrence's at Telscombe, a tiny building characteristic of Downland villages. The nave is largely Norman, but the herring-bone pattern of flints in its south wall dates it from before the Conquest. The timbered roof is also noteworthy. To the south-west, Hangleton Manor is the most important house in Hove, its kitchen dating from 15th century. The cottages to the north were once the gatehouse, and probably joined to the house by a complete courtyard. The main part is 16th century, and contains a 16th-century Screen with the Ten Commandments. Powder closets inserted in the 18th century were cleverly converted into bathrooms in what became an hotel and is now a public house.

Portslade once had a medieval manor house, and there is 12th-century work remaining in the Transitional-Norman Church of St. Nicholas. Old Portslade has tended to be forgotten by conservationists who have recently been discovering several listed buildings, such as the delightful 19th-century Robin's Row cottages, recently restored, an old pub called the Stag's Head, and the ruins of the 12th-century manor house, which were moved closer to St. Mary's Convent in Victorian times. An old brewery and its tall chimney have existed since 1881. The old pitched roof was removed for the addition of a storey. Carbon batteries are now made there. Like the gasometer in Church Road, Hove, it tends to be an eyesore.

Before leaving Brighton, it is essential to take a brief look at another exciting prospect for the town's future. On the 13th July, 1976, details were published about an astonishing £76 million blueprint for the town's centre. The brain-child of the borough planning officer, the scheme will cover the next 15 years, and includes an impressive list of envisaged changes, such as 1,670 houses and flats, 171,000 sq. ft. of shopping, 455,000 sq. ft. of office accommodation, plus an extra 150,600 sq. ft. for light industry. There will be new hotels providing 790 bedrooms, conference centres with 5,500 seats (including the Brighton Centre), a public transport interchange, a bus station, a telecommunications centre, a Post Office sorting office, an extension to Brighton Law Courts, a college of engineering and science, and two community centres. In present inflationary times, it all sounds widly ambitious, and there will be, no doubt, considerable opposition.

Another project to meet with considerable opposition is the mammoth undertaking, known as the Brighton Marina. Conceived in 1966, the original sheme has undergone many amendments.

The Marina's attractions remain basically as originally planned, and are intended to provide for all members of the family, besides those interested in boating. It will be one of the largest independently operating marinas in the world, and certainly the biggest in Europe. The two main breakwaters will enclose a total of 126 acres, the entire area formerly ebbing covered by the sea at high tide.

While the word' "marina" is poetically neat, it cannot convey the scope of this vast undertaking. The best possible conditions will be provided for some 2,300 boats and their owners. It will not, however, be simply an exclusive yacht harbour. Visitors will eventually have a great deal to see and to do. Two breakwaters will provide public promenades, giving unparalleled views of the marina scene, besides enabling extensive angling for the public. Brighton's fishing fleet will have special moorings exclusively for their 14 commercial fishing boats berthed against the east breakwater, off-loading their daily catch in the Marina's boatyard area. By agreement with H. M. Coastguards, there will be a coast-guard station, an inshore rescue service,

148

and a separate emergency rescue service included within the duties of the Marina staff. These emergency services will probably emanate from the Marina's Harbour Control Centre.

Brighton's lifeboat station was established in 1824. Now, the town no longer has a conventional off-shore lifeboat. In 1931, the Royal National Lifeboat Institution closed the station, when the Shoreham and Newhaven lifeboats shared the responsibilities for Brighton. In 1965, the town received its first inshore rescue boat, a 15'6" inflatable craft, fitted with a 40 h.p. outboard engine. The cost of the craft, engine and trailer was £1,000 which was provided by customers of *The Rising Sun*, a London pub. Until 1975, when it was withdrawn at the instigation of the R.N.L.I., the craft was housed 100 yards east of Palace Pier. It was manned by volunteer crews divided into duty watches. In summer they were augmented by beach life guards. Its operational area ranged from Peacehaven in the east to Aldrington Lagoon in the west. Provisional arrangements have now been made between the R.N.L.I. and the Marina Company to site an Atlantic 21-foot lifeboat, with a new crew of local volunteers, within the Marina complex.

If 'something new' applies to Brighton Marina, it will also contain 'something old'. *The Wingfield Castle*, one of the last of the old paddle-steamers, has been berthed at Hull for some time for a survey following its ferry-duties in the Humber. The Marina Company bought her from Sealink, and re-named her 'The Brighton Belle'. This historic 40-year-old is expected to have a permanent home at the Marina, and would form part of the extensive leisure facilities, a floating restaurant being one of her possible uses. Mooring facilities will spread over 77 acres, and will provide excellent berthing, and will include 53 berths for visiting craft. Other marine facilities will include a well equipped boatyard, and one of the largest marine marketing centres for chandlery and equipment in the world.

The public promenade stretches from west to east along the entire length of the Marina's spiral development which divides the harbour waters into two basins and links with two breakwaters. The public will be able to walk along the prmenade, right through the centre of the mooring areas and over the lock gates, so that they will feel closely involved with it all. There will be a multiplicity of shops, cafes, pubs and restaurants, some of which will probably border that promenade. An extensive entertainments complex will cover 400,000 square feet in the western portion of the development, including a large public swimming pool and squash courts and many other facilities, yet to be finalized. It will include Europe's largest marine marketing centre, affording 130,000 square feet of special display premises ashore and commerical moorings for some 170 craft for demonstration and sale. Also, a thrilling water display zone which can provide an extension to the boat exhibition space, a site for a floating bar and restaurant, children's boat trips and a floating concert platform. An underwater bathysphere or submarine experience was also suggested.

Exciting futuristic entertainment is promised in the Cyclorama in the public zone. Its four or five stages will radiate from a central circular stage; the outer circle of auditoria will rotate, moving the entire audience from one audio-visual experience to the next in a journey taken in the same seat. There will be a 500-seat conference hall, also, a circular Dancerama with 360-degree film projection in which a film could be projected all round the audience in a series of day-time performances. In the evening, the Dancerama will make a fabulous dance hall, with discreet visual effects to complement and enhance the music. A unique scene is promised in the sizeable Caribbean Garden, with its smaller swimming pool and tropical plants contained within a controlled climate achieved by glazing. A night club, casino, discothèque and social club are included in the entertainments complex in which the accent is placed on flexibility and multiuse. Add to all this a 500-bedroom hotel, complete with swimming pool and health hydro, and the proposed 850 luxury flats.

The coastline and public undercliff walk will be preserved, and no building will rise above the level of the cliffs, according to the Brighton Marina Parliamentary Act of 1968. In fact, as a result of the second public inquiry, the heights of buildings and spaces between should ensure a most pleasing result. To appreciate the size involved, the Marina spine is equal to the distance from the Brighton Clock Tower — along Western Road — to Norfolk Square, or, for those unfamiliar with Brighton, from Oxford Circus to Piccadilly Circus.

The architect, Mr. David Hodges, FRIBA, has called the Marina "a microcosm of Brighton itself". It is, in reality, a microcosm of *Sussex* itself, and a special gem in the incredible, ageless panorama of the part called East Sussex. Centuries hence, Brighton Marina will probably be standing as an ancient, protected monument to man's ingenuity as he approached the end of the 20th century. By then, some of the old, medieval, heavily-restored churches and other buildings may even have disappeared altogether, to make way for some of the fantastic edifices already envisaged.

Because this may be so, I am closing this chapter with a quotation for those unimaginable times as well as for the exciting ones in which

I have been honoured to traverse so many East Sussex haunts. It is an epitaph, headed "Vulcan", in memory of William Spray, 1788-1878, a local blacksmith. On a tombstone a little distance north-west of Hollington Church-in-the-Wood, it reads:-

> *My hammer and my anvil lie declined,*
> *My bellows, too, have lost their wind,*
> *My fire's extinct, my forge decayed,*
> *and in the dust my vice is laid,*
> *My coal is spent, my iron is gone,*
> *My last nail driven; My work is done.*

PLACES TO VIEW

A brief guide, arranged under broad subject headings, of the most notable natural features of Sussex to which the public has access, and of museums, art galleries, castles, abbeys, houses and other buildings, gardens and wildlife enclosures that are open to the public.

Opening times given are the latest available but, because of constant changes, admission charges are omitted. If, however, no indication is given that admission is free then it should be assumed that a charge is made.

MUSEUMS AND ART GALLERIES

Anne of Cleves House, Lewes. — Sussex ironwork, firebacks, furniture and bygones. For opening times see under "Houses".

Barbican House, Lewes. — Prehistoric, Roman and Saxon exhibits, Sussex pictures and prints. For opening times see under "Houses".

Battle Museum, Old Church House, Battle. — Sussex ironwork, model and plans of Battle of Hastings. Open Easter to October — Weekdays 10.00 to 13.00 and 14.00 to 17.00; Sundays 14.30 to 17.30.

Bexhill Museum, Egerton Park, Bexhill. — Local natural history and archaeology. Open weekdays (except Friday) 10.00 to 17.00. Admission free.

Bluebell Museum, Sheffield Park, nr. Uckfield. — Static railway stock and exhibits. Open from Easter to late October.

Booth Museum, Dyke Road, Brighton. — British birds, birds eggs and lepidoptera. Open weekdays 10.00 to 17.00; Sunday 14.00 to 18.00 (Closes 16.30 in winter.) Admission free.

Brighton Museum and Art Gallery, Church Street, Brighton. — Archaeology, natural history, glass, ceramics, old masters, English watercolours. Open 10.00 to 19.00 Monday to Friday; 10.00 to 17.00 Saturday; 14.00 to 18.00 Sunday. Admission free.

Brighton Pavilion. — Regency furniture and objects d'art. For opening times see under "Houses".

Grange, Rottingdean. — Kipling books and relics; Sussex art and bygones; toy museum. Open 10.00 to 19.00 Monday to Friday; 10.00 to 17.00 Saturday; 14.00 to 17.00 Sunday (to 18.00 in summer). Admission free.

Hastings Museum and Art Gallery, Cambridge Road, Hastings. — Natural history, bygones, ceramics, Sussex iron and pottery, art exhibitions. Open weekdays 10.00 to 13.00; 14.00 to 17.00; Sundays 15.00 to 17.00. Admission free.

Hastings Museum of Local History, Old Town Hall, High Street. — Cinque Port relics, ship models. Open Easter to September weekdays only 9.00 to 12.30; 14.00 to 17.30 (Thursday close 12.30). Admission free.

Preston Manor, Brighton. — Furniture and pictures. For opening times see under "Houses".

R.N.L.I. Museum, Grand Parade, Eastbourne. — Lifeboat equipment plus early lifeboats. Open daily summer 9.30 to 17.00. Spring and autumn — weekends, when weather is suitable. Admission free.

Rye Museum, Ypres Tower, Rye. — Local history, medieval pottery, Victoriana, Cinque Port relics. Open Easter to Mid-October daily 10.30 to 13.00; 14.15 to 17.30. (Open one hour later on Sundays).

Tower 73 (The Wish Tower), Eastbourne. — A restored Martello Tower with historic relics of the Napoleonic period, weapons and documents. Open late May to October daily 10.00 to 17.30. Admission free.

Towner Art Gallery, Borough Lane, Eastbourne. — British painters, Sussex pictures, caricatures, books. Open weekdays 10.00 to 18.00; Sunday 14.00 to 18.00. (Closes 17.00 in winter). Admission free.

Wilmington Priory Museum. — Agricultural and farmhouse implements. Open weekdays (except Friday) April to September 10.00 to 18.00; Sundays 14.00 to 17.00.

Winchelsea Museum, Court Hall, Winchelsea. — Models, maps, documents, handicrafts, Cinque Port relics. Open Whitsun to September.

ABBEYS AND PRIORIES

Battle Abbey. — A Benedictine abbey built by William I to celebrate his victory at Hastings, the high altar marking the spot where Harold fell. Open all the year. Weekdays 10.00 to 13.00; 14.00 to 17.00; Saturdays 10.00 to 12.45. Times vary at Easter and in high season.

Michelham Priory, nr. Hailsham. — An Augustinian foundation of 1229 which became a farmhouse and then home of the Sackvilles for 290 years. Medieval moat, 14th-century gatehouse, tapestries, ironwork, period furniture, stained glass, wagons, musical instruments. Open Easter weekend and May to Mid-October daily 10.00 to 13.00 and 14.00 to 17.30

Robertsbridge Abbey. — Remains of a Cistercian abbey of 1176 incorporated in a farmhouse. The ruins are freely visible — the crypt may be viewed on application at farm.

St. Pancras Priory, Southover, Lewes. — Fragmentary ruins of what was one of the largest monasteries in the country. Founded in 1077 by William de Warenne and his wife Gundrada. The hospitium survives as the parish church of Southover. The ruins are freely visible and the church is open daily.

Wilmington Priory. — A Benedictine priory tucked away under the Downs, 13th century. The ruins are seen, upon application, between 10.00 and 18.00 on weekdays and 14.00 to 17.00 on Sundays. See also under "Museums".

CASTLES

Bodiam Castle. — Built in 1388-9 to protect Sussex against the French but never used. Well preserved and picturesquely reflected in a moat. Splendid example of a medieval castle. Open April to September daily 10.00 to 19.00 and October to March 10.00 to sunset.

Hastings Castle. — Cliff top castle dividing old Hastings from the new. Built by William I. In the ruins is the "Whispering dungeon" and below, in the cliffs, are St. Clements Caves. Open daily 10.00 to 17.30 from Easter to October.

Lewes Castle. — Built just before the Norman Conquest, Lewes is unusual in having two mounds. Now well cared for it has a 14th-century Barbican and a shell keep that was built in 1080 and affords fine views out over the town. Open all the year weekdays 10.00 to 13.00 and 14.00 to 17.30 Also 14.00 to 17.30 on Sundays Easter to September.

Pevensey Castle. — The oldest Sussex castle. Pevensey's walls and towers are built on Roman work and Roman masonry is incorporated. The ruins include Roman walling, round towers, a moat and gatehouse, sally port, towers and dungeons of the 13th century. Open weekdays 9.30 to 19.00 May to September; 9.30 to 19.30

March, April, October and 10.00 to 18.30 November to February. Sundays from 14.00 to times as above.

HOUSES

Anne of Cleves House, Lewes. — Charming 16th-century residence now used as a museum. Open throughout the year February to November weekdays 10.30 to 13.00; 14.00 to 17.30. Easter to September Sundays 14.00 to 17.30.

Barbican House Lewes. — Adjacent to the castle this is a much-altered Elizabethan house, also now used as a museum. Open throughout the year, times as for "Anne of Cleves House".

Batemans, nr. Burwash. — An early 17th-century house in the heart of the Weald. Set in an attractive garden it was Rudyard Kipling's home for 34 years and he described the surroundings of the house in "Puck of Pooks Hill". Open from March to October as follows:- Saturday, Sunday and Good Friday 14.00 to 18.00; Monday, Tuesday, Wednesday and Thursday 11.00 to 12.30 and 14.00 to 18.00

Beeches Farm, nr. Uckfield. — A 16th century tile-hung farmhouse amid delightful gardens. Open daily from 10.00 to 17.00 throughout the year.

Brickwall, Northiam. — A 17th-century timbered house now a school. Rich plaster ceiling in 17th-century drawing room. Open Wednesday and Saturday 14.00 to 16.00 late April to mid-July.

Brighton Pavilion. — One of the most flamboyant buildings in England. Built as the Brighton residence of the Prince Regent by Henry Holland in 1787. Finished in 1822 by Nash in the style of the Moghul palaces of India. State-rooms are in the Chinese manner and the kitchens contain original copperware. During the season all the rooms are furnished to form Britain's finest Regency Exhibition. Open daily throughout the year 10.00 to 17.00.

Charleston Manor, nr. Seaford. — Showing Norman, Tudor and Georgian work, Charleston Manor has an original Norman wing that was referred to in Domesday Book, and was owned by William the Conqueror's cup bearer. It was later inhabited by monks. Now carefully restored the house possesses one of the largest tithe barns in England and this is used for music, literary and art exhibitions. Open 14.15 to 18.00 by appointment only on Wednesdays from mid-May to September.

Firle Place, nr. Lewes. — Nestling at the foot of the Downs this lovely house has been the home of the Gage family for five hundred years. Part Tudor and part Georgian it contains fine furniture,

155

Sevres china and British and European old Masters. Open June to September — Wednesday and Thursday 14.15 to 17.30; Sunday 15.00 to 18.00. Also Easter and Spring Bank Holiday Sundays and Mondays and late summer Bank Holiday 15.00 to 18.00.

Glynde Place, nr, Lewes. — A 16th-century house where Richard Trevor, Bishop of Durham, lived. To him the house owes its stable block and other extensions of 1752. The house has a very fine long gallery and contains paintings by Zoffany, Lely and Rubens. Open 14.15 to 17.30 on Thursday, Saturday and Sunday from May to the end of September and at Easter, spring and late summer Bank Holidays.

Great Dixter, nr. Northiam. — A 15th-century house with a Great Hall of Crutch construction. It was restored by Sir Edwin Lutyens who also designed the gardens. Open Easter to mid-October 14.00 to 17.00 daily (except Monday).

Kidbrooke Park, nr. Forest Row. — This is a beautiful sandstone house that, with its stable block, was built in the 1730's although altered in later years. House and stables open from 14.00 to 16.00 on Monday, Tuesday and Wednesday from August to mid-September.

Lamb House, Rye. — A pleasant Georgian house that was once the home of Henry James. Open from 14.00 to 18.00 on Wednesdays and Saturdays. March to October.

Preston Manor, Brighton. A Georgian house now used as a museum. Open all the year — weekdays 10.00 to 17.00 and Sundays 14.00 to 17.00.

OTHER BUILDINGS AND FEATURES OF INTEREST.

Bluebell Railway. — A 5 mile stretch of the former line from East Grinstead to Lewes built by the L.B.S.C.R. in 1882. Closed in 1958 but re-opened between Horsted Keynes and Sheffield Park in 1960 by an enthusiast group who run passenger trains from March to October. Stock includes locomotives and coaches from many former railway companies. The line crosses from East Sussex into the western area.

Ditchling Cross, nr. Plumpton. — A great Greek-type cross of 100 foot span cut into the Downs above Plumpton. It was cut by monks from Southover (Lewes) some time soon after the Battle of Lewes (in 1264) which was fought on nearby Mount Harry Hill. May be seen freely at all times.

Glyndebourne nr. Lewes. — One of the most beautiful theatres in the world. Glyndebourne was founded in 1934 by Audrey and John

Christie and is attached to a 15th-century house. The opera festival runs from May for a summer season each year and a visit is made more memorable by the pleasure of walking in the lovely gardens in the interval.

Litlington Horse. — A 90 foot long horse cut on the Downs not far from Seaford. May be freely seen at all times.

Long Man of Wilmington. — Most famous hill figure of them all, a huge man carved on the Downs near Wilmington. Renovated in the 19th century, the figure may be Saxon in origin. At 231 feet in height it is said to be largest human figure in the world. May be freely seen at all times.

Mount Caburn nr. Lewes. — Hill top 490 feet high with Iron Age fort on summit. May be freely seen at any time.

Old Mint House, Pevensey. — Said to be on the site of an original Norman Mint, this building was erected in 1432 but later altered. The minting room may be seen. Open daily.

Priest's House, Alfriston, nr. Seaford — Half timbered and thatched this is a priest's or clergy house of 1350. The very first building ever acquired by the National Trust in 1896. Living room open daily during daylight hours. Admission free.

GARDENS

Batemans, nr. Burwash. — Attractive garden with yew hedges, lawns, daffodils. Described by Kipling in "Puck of Pooks Hill". For opening times see under "Houses".

Beeches Farm, nr. Uckfield. — Lawns, borders, yew trees, roses and sunken garden. Fine views. For opening times see under "Houses".

Great Dixter, nr. Northiam. — A beautiful garden that was designed by Sir Edwin Lutyens. Yew hedges and topiary work, plants of horticultural interest, naturalised daffodils and fruitillaries, roses, peonies, primulas, fuchsias, clematis and herbaceous borders. For opening times see under "Houses".

Sheffield Park Gardens, nr. Uckfield. — Famous and beautiful gardens with five lakes, at differing levels, that were first laid out in the 18th century. Rare trees and shrubs are found here as are water lilies, maples and rhododendrons. Open 10.00 to 19.00 on Wednesday, Saturday and Sunday during April; 11.00 to 19.00 daily from May to September and 10.00 to 17.00 during October. Also 11.00 to 19.00 on Easter, Spring and later Summer Bank Holdiays, but not Good Friday.

ZOOS AND WILDLIFE

Brighton Aquarium, Marine Parade, Brighton. — World famous collection of tropical, marine and fresh water fishes, seals, penguins, turtles, large conger eels and, in the new Dolphinarium, dolphins and sea-lions. Open 9.00 to dusk throughout the year.

Drusilla's Children's Zoo, Alfriston. — Birds, and animals, many tame and roaming freely in the enclosure. Llama with young calf. Ornamental waterfowl in the pond. Open 11.00 to 18.00 daily throughout the year. Admission free.

Nap Wood, nr, Frant. — A small nature reserve owned by the National Trust and leased to the Sussex Naturalists Trusts. Predominantly oak trees. Includes a nature trail. Open on Sunday 9.00 to 18.00 from April to October.

Heathfield Wildlife Park. — Privately owned. 450 acres of estate; 200 acres open to the public. Beech and birch woods with many other varieties of trees. Woodland walks and a nature trail. Veteran and vintage car collection. Open 10.00 to 18.00 all the year round.

INDEX

160